Stature and Stigma

Other Books by Henry B. Biller

Father, Child, and Sex Role: Paternal Determinants of Personality Development
Lexington Books, 1971

Paternal Deprivation: Family, School, Sexuality, and Society
Lexington Books, 1974

Father Power, with Dennis L. Meredith
McKay, 1974; Doubleday, paperback edition, 1975

The Other Helpers: Paraprofessionals and Nonprofessionals in Mental Health, with Michael Gershon
Lexington Books, 1977

La Deprivazione Paterna (Italian edition of *Paternal Deprivation*)
Il Pensiero Scientifico, 1978

Parental Death and Psychological Development, with Ellen B. Berlinsky
Lexington Books, 1982

Child Maltreatment and Paternal Deprivation: A Manifesto for Research, Prevention, and Treatment, with Richard S. Solomon
Lexington Books, 1986

Stature and Stigma

The Biopsychosocial Development
of Short Males

Leslie F. Martel
Henry B. Biller
University of Rhode Island

Lexington Books
D.C. Heath and Company/Lexington, Massachusetts/Toronto

To Abby and Maggie

Library of Congress Cataloging-in-Publication Data

Martel, Leslie F.
  Stature and stigma.

  Bibliography: p.
  Includes indexes.
  1. Stature, Short—Psychological aspects.
  2. Stature, Short—Social aspects.   3. Men—Psychology.
  I. Biller, Henry B.   II. Title.
  QP84-M36   1987   155.6'32   86-45937
  ISBN 0-669-14632-3 (alk. paper)

Copyright © 1987 by D.C. Heath and Company

Published simultaneously in Canada
Printed in the United States of America
Casebound International Standard Book Number: 0-669-14632-3
Library of Congress Catalog Card Number: 86-45937

The paper used in this publication meets the minimum requirements of
American National Standard for Information Sciences—Permanence of
Paper for Printed Library Materials, ANSI Z39.48-1984. ♾™

87 88 89 90 8 7 6 5 4 3 2 1

Contents

Figures and Tables

Figures

Tables

Preface

T his book grew out of our long-standing interest in the ways in which biological, family systems, and sociocultural factors interact in the complex processes of personality development. In particular, we have been dismayed at the general lack of acknowledgement of the impact of stature and physique factors in psychology textbooks pertaining to development, personality functioning, and clinical issues. In choosing to focus on the influence of stature on the psychological and social development of males, our goal was to make an initial step toward a holistic-transactional approach.

We are seeking to understand how an individual's relative height interacts with other personal characteristics, family variables, and cultural factors to influence his psychological functioning. We are not arguing that stature is more important than other relatively biologically influenced ingredients or that, in itself, it is more critical than the quality of child-rearing or the individual's socioeconomic background. However, we insist that stature merits equal attention with family and social environment influences especially as it may interact with them in affecting the individual's development.

There certainly has been some attention in the general developmental and clinical literature to the psychological and social handicaps associated with extreme deviations in height and physique such as dwarfism or other conditions caused by clear-cut genetic or endocrinological factors and/or unusually harsh environmental trauma (including severe maltreatment by parents). In many discussions of psychological functioning, there is a sort of compartmentalization of biological and social influences: there is a consideration of stature and some maturational variables, but there is no intergration with other psychosocial developmental processes.

A major goal of the present book is to underscore that even more modest stature deficits among adult males well within the normal distribution, such as being relatively short (e.g., 5'5" or even 5'7" or 5'8"), may be associated with a vulnerability to certain types of psychological difficulties and personality adaptations. On the other hand, other things being equal, tall men appear to have some definite psychological and social advantages compared to men of average height, although their superiority is not as clear-cut as it is when they are compared to short men. Moreover, all males, even those who are tall, have strong values concerning their height and that of others.

Acknowledgments

The previously unpublished data discussed in chapters 5 and 6 came from research we conducted between 1982 and 1986. We are much indebted to the generous cooperation of our participants, especially those who consented to lengthy interview procedures. We wish to express our appreciation to Peter Merenda, Professor Emeritus, University of Rhode Island for his expert guidance in data analysis. Henry Biller's wife, Margery Salter, and sons—Jonathan, Kenneth, Cameron, Michael, and Benjamin—were particularly supportive during the last year of writing this book. Dianne Sipe, Ruth Saunders and Joanne Lawrence displayed much skill and patience in typing various drafts of the manuscript. We were also fortunate to have the interest and enthusiasm of Margaret Zusky, editor at Lexington Books, during various stages of our work. Marsha Finley, production editor, greatly deserves our thanks for the careful shepherding of the manuscript into book form.

1
Stigma and Physical Appearance

I n his now classic work *Stigma*, Goffman (1963) brilliantly analyzed the problems encountered by people with various physical, intellectual, and social handicaps. Discriminatory attitudes and unfair expectations are commonly directed against stigmatized individuals. With regard to physical appearance, unfortunately, many individuals deviate from ideal expectations: Those who are considered ugly, deformed, or extremely obese, for example, may suffer tremendous and tragic social discrimination and personal rejection.

There has been some consideration in the exceptionality and developmental literature of individuals who have suffered from clear-cut biological handicaps relating to severely retarded growth patterns and/or body type and stature deviations. It is apparent that nutritional, genetic, endocrinological, and environmental deprivation (psychosocial) factors can all be major antecedents (in and of themselves or in various combinations) contributing to body type and stature handicaps (Hetherington and Parke 1986, Tanner 1978).

As Hetherington and Parke (1986) emphasize, an individual who is twenty percent or more below average in height at a given age is generally considered to be short, while an individual who is twenty percent or more above the norm is typically labeled tall. Dwarfs (and giants) are those, from a clinical perspective, who deviate more than forty percent from the expected adult height for their sex. Extreme deviations in height are much more common among males, who vary to a greater extent in all physical dimensions than do females (Garai and Scheinfeld 1968).

More than half of very short individuals have no apparent endocrinological or biological abnormality. They seem to be just representatives of the lower end of the normal distribution of height. About twenty-five percent of individuals who are very short as children and adolescents, being late maturers, do tend to catch up to their peers in height (or at least are not as deviant in height) by late adolescence. At least ten percent of very short individuals are clearly the recipients of "short" genes from their parents. Endocrinological disorders, chromosomal abnormalities, and prenatal complications, all of which can be major factors in shortness, may or may not have an inherited genetic basis (Katchadourian 1977, Tanner 1978).

However, deviations from average which are well within the normal range, or deviations from ideal height for a given age, are not usually considered to have any particular psychological consequence by most clinical and developmental researchers. Short men are not a group that is typically viewed in social analyses when categories of handicaps are discussed. Nevertheless, very prevalent and biased cultural attitudes are directed against men of short stature. The following are two dramatic examples of especially negative attitudes toward short men that are attributed to characters from contemporary novels.

> Let me tell you my theory of small men, Captain, then let me hear what you think. . . . Give me a guy less than five feet eight, Johnson, and I'll give you a real bastard nine times out of ten. It has been my experience that short men get a chip on their shoulder as big as an aircraft carrier. They're just pissed off at life and God and everybody else just because they're midgets. They came into the Marine Corps just so they can be proud and tough once in their lives. They like to strut around and pretend their dicks are as long as anyone else's. What do you have to say about my theory? (Colonel Bull Meecham in Pat Conroy's *The Great Santini*, 1976, pp. 165–166.)

> Bond had always mistrusted short men. They grew up from childhood with an inferiority complex. All their lives they would strive to be bigger than others who had teased them as a child. Napoleon had been short, and Hitler. It was the short men that created all the trouble in the world (Ian Fleming, *Goldfinger*, 1959, p. 25).

Body Type

As these quotes highlight, strong notions regarding the relationship between a man's height, behavior, and personality exist. Although most contemporary theorists in the behavioral sciences give little attention to relationships between body type and behavior, historically, there has been considerable lay and professional interest in the relationship between how one looks and how one feels or behaves. Ernst Kretschmer was one of the first researchers to study the relationship between psychopathology and body types. He was convinced that psychopathology could be better understood by increasing our understanding of different body types, and the relationship between temperament and body type. In his classic work *Physique and Character*, Kretschmer (1936) reported a strong correlation between certain types of physical constitutions and particular syndromes of psychological disturbance (e.g., ectomorphy and schizophrenia, endomorphy and manic-depressive disorders). Evidence also links a mesomorphic physique with aggressive acting-out and delinquent behavior (Glueck and Glueck 1956; Hartl, Monnelly and Elderkin 1982).

Sheldon (1940) expanded upon Kretschmer's earlier work and was particularly interested in whether people who had similar bodies behaved in similar ways. Both Kretschmer and Sheldon concluded that physical constitution was of primary importance in the shaping of personality. Basically, Sheldon's method consisted of making predictions about an individual's temperament and preferences by "measuring his body." In his later books, Sheldon (1940, 1954) continued to maintain that physique was a primary factor in personality development. Barker (1953) was another prominent researcher who believed that an individual's physical attributes such as his size, shape, appearance, and strength determined to a great extent the kind of person he became. However, for the most part, during the past thirty years there has been a waning of interest in analyzing behavior as a direct function of physique and appearance. The comparatively few researchers who include measures of body type in their data analyses tend to ascribe relationships of physique to personality as an artifact of stereotypes rather than to the existence of fundamental biological factors.

Even though strong beliefs and opinions exist regarding the relationship between physical stature, behavior, and personality, there is a paucity of methodologically sound research on the topic. Over thirty years ago, Barker (1953) noted that:

> Despite the importance that laymen and social scientists attach to the psychological significance of physique, relatively little has been done to determine systematically the extent to which normal variations in physique actually do influence behavior, and the means by which their effects are accomplished (p. 14).

In referring to the systematic study of short stature in particular, Barker (1953) reported that he was unable to find any investigations on this topic whatsoever. He found this situation curious in light of the fact that short stature was so frequently mentioned in the literature as a liability. In the more than thirty years that have elapsed since his work, the situation has not changed appreciably. Authors who have expressed interest in short stature consistently note how little actual research is available (e.g., Adams 1980, Feldman 1975, Graziano et al. 1978, Keyes 1980). As to why so little research has been conducted on the topic, Keyes speculates:

> I think the whole problem makes everybody nervous all around with short people themselves wishing the issue would just go away, [and] normal sized people often wishing short people would just go away (p. 92).

Remarkable progress has been made in recent years in the area of human height control, making the choice of a particular stature a possible viable option in the near future. Human Growth Hormone, the chemical substance produced by the pituitary gland, can stimulate growth, but its exceedingly limited supply and sometimes dangerous side-effects have severely limited its use. However, recent breakthroughs in genetic engineering promise to make growth hormone available in large quantities at relatively low cost (Gertner 1986, Siegel 1982). Given this remarkable advance, it is essential that the psychosocial impact of short stature be better understood.

The question will soon arise as to whether or not an individual should be given pharmacological treatment for purely psychological reasons. It is certain that technological advances will significantly increase the pressures upon parents, children, and physicians to use the pharmacological approach. Without a better understanding of the impact of short stature, the data base used to assess the costs and benefits of such a powerful intervention remains markedly incomplete.

Physical Attractiveness

> George Bernard Shaw once noted that "Beauty is all very well, but who ever looks at it when it has been in the house three days?" The answer is, almost everybody (Berscheid, Walster, and Bohrnstedt 1973, p. 119).

A Janus-faced American mythology exists regarding the importance of physical appearance: the public one and the private one. The public version asserts that all individuals are treated equally in important life areas regardless of physical appearance. This is congruent with the American ideal of equality. However, the private view of a large proportion of our population seems to be at odds with this assertion and highlights the supreme importance of physical appearance in major social interactions throughout the life cycle. Western media attention to physical appearance dramatizes this point. Elliot Aronson has suggested that social scientists have avoided investigation of the topic because of fear they might learn just how powerful it is (Berscheid 1972, p. 43).

Reviewing the literature on appearance and self-esteem, Berscheid, Walster, and Bohrnstedt (1973) concluded that:

> Personality and self-esteem do not rest exclusively on satisfaction with one's body, but neither is the body an irrelevant shell in which the soul happens to live. We treat beautiful people differently from the way we treat homely ones, and denying this truth will not make a person's looks less important (p. 146).

Berscheid and Walster (1972) reported that subjects preferred physically attractive individuals and that positive personality traits were associated with an attractive appearance. The subjects described the good-looking persons as being more sensitive, kind, interesting, strong, poised, modest, sociable, outgoing, and exciting than less attractive persons.

It is almost axiomatic that short males are not attractive, or at least not as attractive as their taller counterparts. This point is concisely made by the title of an article in *Ms. Magazine*: "Short, Dark and Almost Handsome" (Gross 1975). Emphasis in this article was placed on the "almost."

Body Cathexis

Males and females are different in many aspects of their physical development and socialization history. They also are different in the ways in which they think about and experience their own bodies. The desired shape and size of one's body closely corresponds to the cultural stereotypes; the male desires to be large and muscular while the female desires to be small except for bust area (Calden, Lundy, and Schlafer 1959). More importantly, the symbolic meaning of the body and manner of body cathexis differs for males and females. Jourard and Remy (1957) explored the relationship between the degree of differentiation of self and body image and found that women showed greater variability than did men. Men tended to accept or reject their bodies in a global all-or-none fashion, whereas women made finer-grained distinctions between different aspects of their body. Jourard and Remy concluded that women

> have a more highly differentiated body image than men and that among women, the self-concept and the body image are differentiated to an equivalent degree (p. 63).

These findings were reconfirmed by Kurtz (1969), and Goldberg and Folkins (1974). In Western societies women pay more attention to particular details of their appearance, whereas men are more concerned with the aspects associated with size, strength, and the overall perceptual impact their body makes. A particularly salient dimension that men must deal with in developing an acceptance of their bodies is their relative height. Short men typically have an extremely difficult time forming a sense of physical adequacy and competency.

On the other hand, being overweight and especially being obese is, other things being equal, a greater handicap for women than it is for men. Femininity is often associated with petiteness and, at the very least, being large is seen as unfeminine whether it is being very tall or overweight. It is interesting to note in this context that eating disorders are much more prevalent among women than they are among men: In general women have a much greater concern with the implications of their being overweight than do men (Wishon et al. 1983).

Some men who perceive themselves as being short actually try to make themselves heavier, build themselves up, as a compensation for being short. Clinical interviews have revealed that some men feel it is better to take up a significant amount of space: even though they can't make themselves taller, they can make themselves bigger (Martel and Biller 1986). It should be emphasized, of course, that the short, broad, and muscular male is generally perceived in a much more favorable light than is the short, fat male although both are clearly at a disadvantage compared to their taller counterparts who are also well-built.

Ideal Body Type

It is essential to emphasize that large body size has a symbolic meaning to males that is unique to their gender. Fisher (1973) pointed out that the shape and size of the body is imbued with special and important meaning. To be a tall and nonobese male is a highly valued physical characteristic. The inculcation of this ideal occurs early in development. In his study, Cobb (1954) reported that children emphatically believed that a tall, muscular physique was important for boys. This cultural ideal is linked with symbolic meaning that indicates to those who are less than ideal that they have somehow fallen short of an important mark. As Fisher (1973) succinctly summed it up:

> All other things being equal, the large man is viewed as more manly. We know that tall men tend to get better paying jobs than short ones, presumably because they make a more forceful impression. It has been said that the short man feels inferior and is sometimes driven to do big, masculine things in order to prove his true size (p. 119).

Given such a set of environmental circumstances, stereotyping, and cultural expectations, it is clear that a myriad of difficulties confronts the short male in terms of negotiating and solidifying a positive male identity.

The consensus regarding the physical appearance that a male should have is unequivocal. The ideal favors a large mesomorphic body type that is expected to be strongly associated with masculine characteristics. This expectation has profound developmental and personality implications for the male of short stature. Discussing physical appearance and peer relations, Berscheid et al. (1972) concluded that "it seems that childhood teasing has a lasting effect. People who were teased as children . . . are less satisfied with their bodies as adults . . . and the relationship between having been made fun of as a child and later body image was stronger for males than for females" (p. 122).

Body Satisfaction

Hinckley and Rethlingshafer (1951) found that the men who were most satisfied with their own height were the 6'2" subjects, and the least satisfied individuals were those who were unusually short. The relationship between perceived masculinity and size of various bodily characteristics was tested by Jourard and Secord (1954). They had college males complete the Body Cathexis Scale. After the subjects completed the scale, body measurements were taken (i.e., height, weight, width of shoulders, circumference of the biceps), and correlations between these measurements and the pertinent body cathexis ratings were computed. The results indicated that large size of relevant body parts was associated with positive cathexis while the reverse was true for small size. There was a clear relationship between possessing large bodily characteristics and positive attitudes toward one's own body.

In a replication of Secord and Jourard's (1953) work, Magnussen (1958) also had male undergraduate subjects complete a form of the Body Cathexis Scale. Upon completion of the Body Cathexis Scale, anthropometric measurements were taken on each subject for height, weight, shoulder width, and chest circumference. Magnussen found that large size was a clearly desirable attribute among college males, and "the presence or absence leads to contrasting feelings toward related features of the male soma" (p. 34).

Jourard and Secord (1955) found that "cathexis for selected body aspects will vary with the extent of deviation perceived and measured size of body parts for self-ratings of ideal measurements" (p. 243). Calden, Lundy, and Schlafer (1959), using the same line of reasoning, asked male college students to fill out a questionnaire that asked for estimates of the size of various body features and statements as to the extent of satisfaction with these features. The results again confirmed that males distinctly prefer largeness of bodily proportions, especially with regard to stature. Of the males who voiced dissatisfaction with their body features, all but two of them wished to be taller.

Gunderson (1965) obtained self-ratings of various body areas from navy enlisted men. He found an almost perfect linear relationship between satisfaction with one's height and the extent to which it approximated the cultural ideal of 6'2". Those who were either too short or too tall were the most dissatisfied with their height. Gunderson concluded that height appeared to have a pervasive effect upon self-evaluation. The short underweight and short overweight groups had the most unfavorable self-image.

Arkoff and Weaver (1966) examined body image and body dissatisfaction among Caucasian and Japanese-American college students using the Body Cathexis Questionnaire. They found that both the Caucasian and Japanese-American males wanted to be large in all of the dimensions under study except for their hips and waist. As was hypothesized, the Japanese-Americans, who were shorter, were further from their ideal in terms of height and bicep size and seemed to be less accepting of their bodies. The authors concluded that the dimensions of height and upper body shape (i.e., the classic tall mesomorphic build) symbolize masculinity in the American culture. This ideal is generally accepted and aspired toward by males, and it cuts across different sociocultural groupings.

The findings from various research studies are strikingly consistent and have profound implications for understanding the psychology of the short male. A man's body image is based, to a very large extent, on how closely a few of his physical dimensions approximate the stereotypic cultural standard. The manner in which the body is cathected appears to be substantially different between the sexes, with males putting much more emphasis on size and females having a more differentiated view including many different bodily details.

In an early study of masculine inadequacy and compensatory development of physique, Harlow (1951) noted:

> Since the male, in almost all societies, is the sex expected to be strong and dominant, the given physical sex difference can easily become a symbol for male superiority. It follows that the more highly developed are the secondary masculine characteristics, the more manly the individual is often considered (p. 313).

In an interview published in *Playboy*, the very successful songwriter Paul Simon (1984) articulated the essence of this perceived relationship between physical size and manliness. When the interviewer asked him what role being short had played in his life, he replied:

> I think it had the most significant single effect on my existence, aside from my brain. In fact, it's part of an inferior–superior syndrome. I think I have a superior brain and an inferior stature, if you really want to get brutal about it (p. 172).

All in all, men value bigness of body parts, and it appears that much of the role of being a man is inextricably interwoven with the notion of bigness. Developmentally, males test themselves based on this physical dimension, and if they do not measure up they often have difficulty competing in sports and succeeding in heterosexual involvements. The symbolic meaning of the body to the male is different than that for the female, that is, the male must have a body that can offer physical security to self and others. If the male is unable to meet this challenge, the expression of this failure may emerge as a defensive psychological stance.

Preview

The next three chapters go into more depth about what is known concerning the personality and social adjustment of the short male. Chapter 2 focuses on dimensions of personality functioning including defensive styles, self-concept, and self-esteem. Chapter 3 surveys research relating to developmental issues in childhood including timing of physical maturation, adolescent conflicts, and factors in early heterosexual relationships. Chapter 4 deals with the role of stature in the broader social context and summarizes data pertaining to body stereo-typing, status, and vocational discrimination.

The last two chapters are based on a rather extensive investigation of the influence of relative height on the perceptions and personality adaptations of male college students. Chapter 5 presents analyses of questionnaire, body perception, semantic differential, and self-concept measures. Chapter 6 provides an integration and overview of the data in conjunction with previous research while also highlighting the results of in-depth interviews with short males.

We use a holistic-transactional framework in our attempt to understand the influence of relative stature on the personality development of males. There is certainly much stress on the learning of stereotypes and the cultural attribution of specific characteristics to men of different heights. However, we also acknowledge that there is a biosocial substrate which provides for certain interpersonal predispositions regardless of particular family or cultural settings (Biller and Solomon 1986). There are, other things being equal, inherent disadvantages in being much smaller and shorter than one's peers. Such disadvantages typically range from lesser strength and physical leverage to more subtle social handicaps relating to level of eye contact and spatial submissiveness.

Biosocial predispositions relating to shortness and difficulties in peer competition in childhood may appear far removed from adult interactions, but such experiences are important in molding long-lasting attitudes and self-perceptions. The short male has to cope with being different and being at a disadvantage. How much of a handicap shortness remains depends on a myriad of biologically connected, as well as family and sociocultural, factors. The interactions of such factors as body type, timing of maturation, intellectual resources, parental acceptance, paternal influence, peer values, and socioeconomic status must all be taken into account in order to understand the way in which an individual may deal with a potential handicap (Biller and Solomon 1986).

2
Stature and Personality Functioning

Considering the potential importance of the link between stature and personality, there has been extremely little direct research on the topic. In an early review of available evidence, Barker (1953) concluded that there was solid evidence for the correlation between positive (i.e., good, valued, and approved of) characteristics and physical size.

Hood (1963) examined the Minnesota Multiphasic Personality Inventory (MMPI) profiles of groups representing extremes of height and weight. The subjects were drawn from a large college student population at the University of Minnesota. In this study, the entering male freshmen who were sixty-five inches or shorter, and those who were seventy-five inches or taller, were compared with each other and a general student population sample. Hood found that the short males scored slightly but significantly higher than extremely tall subjects on the inferiority and depression scales of the MMPI. The findings indicated that feelings of inferiority and depression were inversely related to height.

Adams (1980) studied adult men and women to assess personality differences that could possibly be attributed to physical characteristics. Extended interviews were conducted which included gathering information relating to locus of control, assertiveness, intelligence, emotionality, and responsibility. Subjects were also questioned about their social behavior including degree of social involvement, perceived social satisfaction, and social interaction. Height was found to be positively associated with sensation seeking, likeableness, and self-directive locus of control, and negatively correlated with emotional expression and the belief in luck or chance in directing one's life. Taller individuals were found to be less emotionally reactive and experienced themselves as being more in control of what happened to them in life.

Although the number of studies is quite meager, research that directly assesses the relationship between height and psychological functioning points to the possibility that physical characteristics such as size may account for a significant portion of the variance in the complex equation of personality development.

Defensive Style

> It is as if a man feared that he was too small and walked on his toes to make himself seem taller. Sometimes we can see this very behaviour if two children are comparing their height. The one who is afraid that he is smaller will stretch up and hold himself very tensely. He will try to seem bigger than he is. If we asked such a child, "Do you think you are too small?", we should hardly expect him to acknowledge the fact (Adler 1956, p. 260).

Alfred Adler (1956) believed that the desire to obtain power was a central motivating force in a person's life. Based on this supposition, he postulated that people who feel that they are not quite adequate on a physical level may develop an inferiority complex. Adler introduced the term "Napoleon Complex" when discussing men who defensively dealt with inferiority feelings connected to short stature. Adler believed that attitudes about the adequacy of bodily characteristics play a crucial role in determining our entire psychological development. Both Freud and Adler maintained that feelings about our bodies are to a great extent stored in the unconscious regions of our minds (Gillis 1982).

Wilhelm Reich (1945) coined the concept of "body armor" to describe the defensive posture individuals take in confronting their social environment. He emphasized that we use our body as a protective sheath to deal with potentially conflicting and anxiety provoking interactions with others. The individual who feels physically inadequate may be at a special disadvantage in dealing with others, particularly because of feelings of vulnerability and fear of rejection. Such individuals are especially likely to develop very rigid body armor.

The short male is frequently reminded that his body is inferior. For example, he may experience much difficulty in finding clothing, or he may be unable to sit comfortably in many public places, including bars and restaurants (Feldman 1975). A particularly poignant experience for the short male is to find himself in a situation where seemingly normal seating arrangements emphasize his inability to have his feet reach the floor. A person's chronic dissatisfaction with his body may lead to adoption of compensatory mechanisms. Adler (1956) stressed:

> No human being can bear a feeling of inferiority for long; he will be thrown into a tension which necessitates some kind of action. But suppose an individual is discouraged; suppose he cannot conceive that if he makes realistic efforts he will improve the situation. He will still be unable to bear his feelings of inferiority; he will still struggle to be rid of them; but he will try methods which bring him no farther ahead . . . his feelings of inferiority will accumulate, because the situation which produces them remains unaltered. The provocation is still there. Every step he takes will lead him farther into self-deception, and all of his problems will press in upon him with greater and greater urgency (pp. 258–259).

In regard to development, each individual must come to terms with the body that he inhabits. Fisher (1973) points out that

> each person in the world has to learn how to feel secure in that most funda-
> mental home base of all, his body. He has to develop confidence that the walls
> of his body can adequately shield him from all potentially bad things "out there"
> (p. 20).

If an individual does not successfully negotiate this most fundamental task, Fisher believes, there is a possibility that he will seek compensatory ways of reaffirming his own body boundaries. A sense of physical adequacy is a particularly important core dimension in masculine development because of the traditional em-
phasis on the male's ability to be physically assertive or protective of others, including females (Biller 1971).

If a sense of bodily vulnerability develops, its effects may have long-term developmental consequences. Kagan and Moss (1964) studied the connections be-
tween bodily related perceptions at different developmental stages for subjects involved in the Fels Research Institute Longitudinal Study. The subjects were rated during childhood with regard to fear of bodily injury, the presence of irrational fears, avoidance of dangerous play, and the degree to which they were disturbed by injury and illness. Kagan and Moss (1962) found that:

> The boys who showed evidence of intense physical harm anxiety during
> the preschool years, were, as adults, anxious about sexuality, uninvolved in
> traditionally masculine activities, and highly concerned with intellectual com-
> petence and status goals (p. 191).

While the Kagan and Moss (1962) research did not directly address the role of short stature, it did underscore that a flight from the body world may be accompanied by an increasingly cerebral approach to life. This may be of some importance in understanding the personality of the short male. In an interview study, Martel and Biller (1986) noted that there may be a significant socioeconomic and subcultural difference in the way short males manage their shortness, with lower socioeconomic status groups becoming more physically aggressive and upper middle-class groups becoming more cerebral in their approach to life. The short male generally exists in a social milieu where aggressive physical assertiveness is considered to be a hallmark of a masculine approach to the world. Yet to act in such a manner could be physically dangerous for the small male. Keyes (1980) emphasized that unlike larger individuals,

> smaller people . . . throughout their life are reminded that they'd better be care-
> ful or they might get hurt. Implicit in such reminders is the lesson that physical
> well-being in the presence of larger bodies can depend on the ability to be
> agreeable (p. 286).

Fisher and Cleveland (1968) made some provocative comments about the different styles one can use in handling angry impulses:

> In such situations there is a conflict between wanting to express the anger in an aggressive self-determined fashion and fear of the consequences of being aggressive. . . . The individual who reacts to conditions of frustration simply by becoming anxious or blaming himself is adopting an orientation quite the opposite of what one should associate with a lifestyle built around active mastery and structuring of the environment (p. 132).

Evidence for such processes is often suggested in the comments of very short men. For example, five-foot-tall songwriter Paul Williams explained the development of his comic sense of humor by saying that if one were humorous "they weren't going to punch you" (Keyes 1980, p. 288). Five-foot-four actor Dudley Moore also learned to negotiate his way in the world through the use of humor. He says of this: "People like to laugh, and they love those who can make them do so" (Moore 1983, p. 70).

Using humor to reduce personal anxiety and gain acceptance is often characteristic of the short male. It has in fact been called the "clowning or mascot-adaptational response" (Finch 1978). Evidently, many short males feel that it was essential for them to develop such a defensive style as a matter of psychological and physical survival. Actor Joel Grey, who is very short, replied in regard to this supposition that it was

> "how I used to get out of fights with guys who were a lot bigger," Grey recalled. "I'd use my humor." He smiled, but the smile slowly dissolved and finally disappeared. Grey shook his head, adding "not good." "What's not good about humor for survival," he continued, "is that you end up not really saying what you feel to the person because they're a danger. And you don't feel good about yourself because you've copped out, so to speak, when actually what you've done is to be practical" (Keyes 1980, p. 102).

Some research data indicate that individuals with poor body images avoid physical activities and tend to gravitate to intellectual endeavors. Sperling (1975) studied the leisure activity preferences of adolescents as they related to body image. He administered a leisure activity preference questionnaire and analyzed the Draw-A-Person test to measure body image. He found that students who were most involved in intellectual activities had the lowest body image scores. He concluded that those with poor body images avoided athletic activities while giving an increasing amount of time to intellectual tasks. There are individuals who have a positive body image and also are strongly involved in intellectual activities, but the overall negative relationship reported by Sperling is striking.

Fisher (1973) also described individuals who are uncomfortable with their body images as being likely to seek out intellectual outlets. Such individuals, Fisher believes, will flee from the body world into intellectual endeavors. According to Fisher, "a successful career as a student calls for endless hours of sitting (with body almost immovable) while absorbing information from books. The body is largely superfluous to the whole scholastic enterprise" (p. 15). Studious individuals generally attach low importance to feelings related to general body and muscular involvement. It is interesting to speculate about the developmental sequences of such an adaptation. For example, do certain body types (e.g., ectomorphy), as Sheldon might suggest, predispose an individual toward sedentary and intellectual activities, or do individuals withdraw from physical activities because of a sense of failure in physical competition?

Self-Concept and Body Image

An individual's perception of his body occupies a unique place in the world of object perception. This is so because his body is both an instrument of perception and is part of the perception. Fisher (1973) emphasized that body image may frequently serve as a screen or target upon which an individual projects significant personal feelings, anxieties, and values. He explains that

> there is an unusually intense level of ego involvement evoked by one's body as an object of perception. When an individual reacts to his own body, he is stirred and aroused in a manner that rarely occurs when he reacts to the non-self world (p. 49).

An impressive body of evidence underscores the significance of body image in the development of self-concept (e.g., Fisher 1970, 1973; Wylie 1961, 1974; Zion 1965).

Results linking body image and self-concept have extremely important implications for the study of the psychosocial impact of short stature. The body is an anchor point for the concept of the self (Secord and Jourard 1953). The short male's body may not provide him with a solid basis upon which to build a secure self-concept. Body image is the most fundamental dimension of self-concept, and perceived defects in this area are extremely difficult for the individual to overcome. Whether a person feels that

> his body is big or small, attractive or unattractive, strong or weak tells us a good deal about his self-concept or his typical manner of relating to others (Fisher 1964, p. 520).

Freud (1924) emphasized that the concept of the self was basically a body ego construct. Other psychoanalytic theorists have not failed to take note of this as exemplified by Fenichel's (1945) statement that

> to the simultaneous occurrence of both outer tactile and inner sensory data, one's own body becomes something apart from the rest of the world and thus

the discerning of self from non-self is made possible. The sum of the mental representations of the body and its organs, the so-called body image, constitutes the idea of I and is of basic importance for the further formation of the ego (pp. 35–36).

There is a well-established research literature supporting the notion that the way an individual feels about his body will have substantial influence over the way he feels about the self. An unfavorable body image will severely undermine positive feelings toward the self.

From an empirical perspective, such a relationship was first articulated by Secord and Jourard (1953). In their pioneering studies, they developed a scale defining body cathexis as "the degree of feeling of satisfaction or dissatisfaction with various parts or processes of the body" (p. 343). They predicted that they would find a relationship between an individual's feelings about his self and his body. In addition, they hypothesized that a relationship existed between negative feelings about the body and insecurity involving the self. Their predictions were strongly supported by data they collected for both male and female college students. Jourard and Secord (1954) examined the relationship between actual measured size of body characteristics and body cathexis. For college men, large size was generally associated with strong positive feelings while small size was associated with a weak or negative self-concept. Weinberg (1960) reported that lower scores on the body and self cathexis scales were related to feelings of insecurity, and this relationship was of great magnitude for men.

Rosen and Ross (1968) refined the Jourard and Secord assessment techniques somewhat by examining whether or not the reported relative importance of particular parts of the body would affect the correlation between self-concept and body cathexis. They found that self-concept scores were much more positively correlated with body cathexis scores derived from the ratings of body parts viewed as having high importance than with cathexis scores on body parts seen as having low importance. Darden's (1972) research also led to the conclusion that "it appears that the confidence an individual has in his body is related to the confidence with which he faces the self and the world" (p. 7).

Lerner (1973) studied the relationship between physical attractiveness, body attitudes, and self-concept. He found that there were consistent attitudes about the importance of certain body characteristics, and that body satisfaction was clearly related to self-concept. Using the Multiple Affect Adjective Checklist as a measure of body cathexis, Goldberg and Folkins (1974) found that body image was negatively correlated with anxiety, depression, and hostility. Individuals with a poor body image were more prone to anxiety, depression, and hostility than were those with positive body images.

Male children and adolescents who have unmasculine physiques are more likely to have a poor self-concept (Biller and Borstelmann 1967, Biller and Liebman 1971). In an analysis of different aspects of sex-role development, Biller (1974) also stressed that:

> A boy can have a masculine orientation and preference but be limited in the development of a masculine adoption by an inadequate or inappropriate physical status. For example, a boy who is very short or very thin would seem to be at a disadvantage. Height and muscle mass seem positively related to masculinity of sex role adoption. Though a particular type of physique is not sufficient to provide masculine behavior, a boy who is tall and broad or broad though short is better suited for success in most masculine activities than a boy who is tall and thin or short and thin (p. 18).

Self-Esteem

The way an individual feels about himself is reflected by his level of self-esteem. The research indicates that self-esteem, like self-concept, is related to an individual's level of satisfaction with his own body. Self-esteem may be defined within a context of self-other orientation. According to Ziller (1973) the individual's self-esteem is based on paired comparisons of the self and significant others. His own self-evaluation develops and is maintained within a social frame of reference. The short male is consistently confronted with a social (and physical) frame of reference that emphasizes a dramatic discrepancy between his height and that of other males of similar age and status.

In a study that highlights this point, Prieto and Robbins (1975) emphasized the powerful effect others have on an individual's self-esteem. Male junior high school students, ages twelve to fifteen, were administered a battery of tests including an estimate of relative height. It turned out that the teacher's evaluation of a student's height had a higher correlation with self-esteem than did the student's own self-evaluation of his height. The researchers concluded that

> there is evidence not only that an individual's self-perceptions of this physical characteristic is related to his self-esteem, but also that perceptions of an individual's height by significant others contributes to this (p. 397).

The Prieto and Robbins results fit well with Wylie's (1961) assertion that aspects of the physical self which significant others devalue undermine self-regard.

Berscheid and Walster (1972) found that for both males and females, body image was closely tied to self-esteem. In this study, only eleven percent of those individuals with below average body image scores were found to have above average levels of self-esteem. The men who were most dissatisfied with their bodies also tended to be the ones who felt most uncomfortable around other men, once again emphasizing the social-evaluative nature of self-esteem.

Men, it appears, are particularly sensitive to the social-evaluative aspects of self-esteem. A man's sense of competence is greatly threatened if he perceives his body as inadequate. Gunderson (1965) studied a population of navy enlisted men ages seventeen to twenty-one and measured their attitudes toward the self and body on the basis of their responses to the Body Cathexis Scale. The influence of social norms upon the men's self-evaluations was evident in that deviations from the ideal height (seventy-two inches) in either direction resulted in increasing dissatisfaction. Gunderson pointed out that

> The cultural ideal for body size appears to be slightly larger than actual body size for this population. Many young adult males apparently find small body size a threat to self-esteem and tend to depreciate their own personal worth based upon this perception (p. 906).

Gunderson (1965) also concluded that physical characteristics "play a significant part in self-evaluation and that research in the area of self-concept or self-regard should take the 'real' characteristics of persons into account" (p. 906).

In essence, available research supports the existence of a strong connection between an individual's feelings toward the self and his body. Developmentally, an individual's inability to become firmly anchored or secure with regard to feelings of body adequacy will have long-term implications for the way in which he interacts with others. The negative feelings associated with a poor body image may lead to a more generalized discomfort involving the self, with consequent ramifications for personality development. Small body size seems to have an especially powerful influence on the development of self-concept among males.

Being short, in itself, is not directly associated with serious psychopathology. Other things being equal, the short male is more likely to experience feelings of physical deficiency and inferiority than are his taller counterparts, but his personal resources and his family support system can be important factors in enabling him to achieve a very positive psychosocial adjustment. Of course, some short males have additional handicaps to contend with and/or may have inadequate parents. It is interesting to note that a lawyer representing a 5' male client accused of a serious felony was "planning an insanity defense based on the traumatic effects of growing up short" (*Newsweek*, October 13, 1986, p. 10).

3
Stature and Psychosocial Development

vailable research pertaining to the emotional, behavioral, and personality development of the short male is sparse but consistent. The literature strongly supports the hypothesis that childhood and adolescence are difficult times for the short male and that the effects of developmental
conflicts are long-lasting.

From the earliest stages of development, so much of parent, family, and
other adult communication directed toward the child or spoken in his presence
relates to size and growth. Much positive feedback (e.g., "what a big boy you
are," "look how much he's grown," "he'll be bigger than his brother soon") as
well as negative feedback (e.g., "eat your vegetables or you won't grow up to be
big and strong," "he's small for his age," "what a little baby you are") revolves
around relative size issues and is often conveyed in an emotionally charged manner. Even in the first few months of life, and continuing throughout the preschool years and later childhood, it is very clear that every individual receives
a vast multitude of messages emphasizing that big and tall relate to goodness
whereas small and short are much less desirable and indeed, often represent an
especially defective condition. Negative communications regarding shortness are
an important part of the social environment that the much smaller than average
boy must continually deal with during his development.

A medical school thesis by Ellen Finch (1978) at Yale described issues relating to the clinical assessment of very short stature in children and adolescents.
In her study eighty-four percent of the subjects were at or below the third per-
centile in height for children of their age. Nearly three times as many boys were
presented for evaluation of short stature, reflecting the greater concern that parents have for growth patterns of their male children (and also the greater variability in the heights of boys than girls).

Finch reported the situations in which the concerns of short children, ages
eight to fourteen, were frequently expressed. The children described difficulty
associated with peer teasing, symptoms such as crying and fighting, and the
clowning or mascot-adaptational response. The parents of these children were
concerned because their short children often preferred the company of playmates

who were three to four years younger. The short boys were particularly distressed because they could not compete successfully in sports. One boy viewed himself as having been "physically and psychologically injured" (p. 80) by his short stature. The onset of adolescence was found to be an especially difficult time, with more than one-third of all the boys ages fourteen to eighteen stating that their relative lack of growth was a major source of distress for them. Finch concluded by stating that " . . . any child who is consistently perceived by others to be younger than his years is clearly susceptible to abnormal personality development" (p. 81).

An impressive body of family research is emerging from the study of the psychosocial development of young children with unusually short stature (e.g., Meyer-Bahlburg 1985; Rotnem 1984). We discuss some of the clinical implications of this research in chapter 6.

Early and Late Maturers

There has been little direct emphasis on the developmental assessment of the psychological and social impact of short stature in males, but there has been research assessing the behavioral and personality differences between late and early maturers. Although some late maturers may eventually attain above average stature, it is essential to note that there is a strong and positive relationship between being a late maturer and being very short (Dwyer and Mayer 1968, Siegel 1982, Tanner 1970, Weatherly 1964).

For example, Weatherly (1964) describes the late maturing boy as having "relatively small immature stature," Dwyer and Mayer (1968) refer to the late maturer's "lack of physical growth," and Tanner (1970) describes the late maturer as "inhabiting the world of the small boy." In essence, the late maturer is, more often than not, the boy of short stature, and findings from this literature are relevant for the understanding of the development of the short boy.

From a historical perspective, there has been a long-standing belief that physical appearance is correlated to maturational level. Baldwin (1921), a pioneer in the study of physical growth over sixty years ago, wrote:

> Physiological age is, the writer believes, directly correlated with the stages of mental maturation. . . . The physiologically more mature child has different types of emotions, and different interests, from the child who is physically younger though of the same chronological age (quoted in Gates, 1924, p. 329).

Even so, if the information is readily available, judgements and expectations of children are typically based on their chronological age. The quip "act your age, not your shoe size" reveals the dilemma the small boy might have. In fact, it is important to emphasize that an individual who is chronologically age four-

teen could either be preadolescent, midadolescent, or postadolescent. For example, as Tanner (1970) in his provocative chapter on physical growth writes,

> . . . it is ridiculous to consider all these three boys as equally grown up . . . since
> much behavior at this age is conditioned by physical stature. . . . The statement
> that a boy is fourteen is in most contexts hopelessly vague (p. 86).

The research assessing the impact of early and late maturational development among boys has yielded strikingly consistent findings. Mussen and Jones
(1957) studied seventeen-year-old males who were selected on the basis of their
physical maturity status. The subjects were part of a normal sample of ninety
boys who were participating in a longitudinal study. Mussen and Jones hypothesized that more of the late maturers, as compared to the early maturers, would
score high in variables related to "negative self-conceptions, dependence, aggression, affiliation, rebelliousness, and feelings of being diminished and rejected"
(p. 244). It was their view that adult and peer attitudes toward the boys as well
as treatment and acceptance would be related to their physical status. In this
study, personality structure was measured by means of the Thematic Appercep-
tion Test.

The results of the Mussen and Jones study supported the hypothesis that
boys whose physical development is retarded are exposed to a sociopsychological
environment that is quite different from that of boys who are early maturers.
Generally, the early maturing boy presented a highly favorable personality pic-
ture with regard to important social variables. Mussen and Jones concluded that
the social environment of the late maturer may have adverse effects on his personality development. The late maturer was in a disadvantageous competitive
position in athletic activities and was treated as immature by others, which could
lead to

> negative self-conceptions, heightened feelings of rejection by others, prolonged
> dependency needs, and rebellious attitudes toward parents. Hence, the physi-
> cally retarded boy is more likely than his early maturing peer to be personally
> and socially maladjusted during his late adolescence (p. 252).

Mussen and Jones (1957) did not assess possible mitigating factors such as
above average intellectual functioning or special talents. Washburn (1962) has
noted that a secure family environment may be a positive factor that alleviates,
to some extent, the disadvantages of being a late maturing boy. Biller (1974) also
reported that young boys who had unmasculine physiques, including those who
were short and thin, were at a particular disadvantage when they grew up in
homes in which the father was absent, whereas those who had relatively mesomorphic physiques and who had above average intellectual development
seemed to be much less impaired by the influence of paternal deprivation.

Jones and Bayley (1950) compared boys who were maturationally retarded during a four-and-one-half year period, beginning at the average age of fourteen, with those who were early maturers. The early maturers were rated as superior in physical attractiveness, were more mesomorphic, and experienced more rapid growth in height. The late maturers were more concerned with attention getting than the early maturers, consistently displaying less socially competent behavior. Jones and Bayley speculated that the small boy may be acting in such a manner because this is "the only technique he knows to hold the attention of others and to compensate for his physically less favored status" (p. 145). Compared to the late maturers, the early maturing boys were more athletically involved, held many important school offices, and generally occupied more prestigious positions in peer and school activities. For example, "two of the sixteen early maturing boys became student body presidents, one was president of the boys club, and several were elected to committee chairmanships and four attained outstanding reputations as athletes. Of the sixteen late maturing boys, only one attained an office (class vice president)" (p. 146). The conclusion that early maturation is associated with clear-cut advantages is well-founded. "If a group of adolescents who do not know one another is asked to select a leader, the group tends to choose a large boy, and shorter adolescents are well aware of this" (Dwyer and Mayer 1968, p. 365).

In other research, Mussen and Jones (1958) studied the "behavior-inferred motivation" of late and early maturing boys. Behavior-inferred motivation means that underlying drives are inferred from observable behavior. The subjects in this study were the same physically accelerated and physically retarded boys who were evaluated in the previous Mussen and Jones (1957) research. The investigators found that there were distinct differences between the early and late maturers in the social behavior sphere. Even though the late maturers were highly motivated toward social affiliation, the ways in which they went about it were seen as childish and affected. The high social drives of the late maturers seemed to be based on general emotional insecurity which was reflected by tenseness, impulsiveness, and higher dependency needs. Mussen and Jones concluded that physical retardation may be a major factor adversely affecting personality development.

Weatherly (1964) classified 234 male and 202 female college students into groups of early, average, and late maturers and then compared them on a number of personality measures. The subjects were about two years older than the subjects studied by Mussen and Jones (1958). In addition, in the Weatherly research, several objective personality measures were used whereas only the Edwards Personal Preference Schedule was available in the Mussen and Jones investigation. Weatherly found that late physical maturation represented a distinct handicap to the personality development of boys but that these effects were less profound for girls. In agreement with other researchers, Weatherly concluded that the psychosocial environment is more stressful for late maturers, especially males, because they must enter junior or senior high school "with the liability of a relatively small immature physical stature" (p. 1198).

Weatherly described the process of a circular feedback loop in which the environment of the late maturer is one that is "conducive to feelings of inadequacy, insecurity, and defensive 'small boy' behavior" (p. 1198). As part of the transactional feedback loop, others expect more of the taller well-developed male. When cognitive cues, such as the knowledge of a child's age, conflict with perceptual cues, such as the child's perceived height, the latter is the greater determinant of adult expectations for a child's achievement (Brackbill and Nevill 1981). In his research with kindergarten-age children, Biller (1968) also noted that parents of tall, broadly built, mesomorphic boys seem to expect more masculine behavior from them.

As Weatherly (1964) pointed out, many other studies using different procedures, measures, and subjects have all arrived at the same conclusion that the late maturing boy is at a distinct disadvantage in social development as compared to his taller peers. Tanner (1970) summed up this situation concisely:

> The world of the small boy is one where physical prowess brings prestige as well as success, where the body is very much an instrument of the person. Boys who are advanced in development, not only at puberty but before as well, are more likely than others to be leaders. Indeed this is reinforced by the fact that muscular, powerful boys on average mature earlier than others and have an early adolescent growth spurt. The athletically built boy not only tends to dominate his fellows before puberty, but by getting an early start, he is in a good position to continue the domination (p. 92).

Adolescence Issues

The onset of adolescence brings with it an increasingly acute awareness for the small boy that compared to his peers, he is noticeably different in important and disapproved ways. An essential developmental task of adolescence is the acceptance of the body as the symbol of self, and this is something that may be especially difficult for the short boy to do.

Adolescence presents challenges and difficulties for all those passing through this stage of development, but it is a particularly painful time for those who are perceived as being substantially different and deficient in some important way. In adolescence, the individual is acquiring an increasingly differentiated sense of the psychological and physical self, and the very phenomenon of physical growth becomes invested with great symbolic meaning (Dwyer and Mayer 1968). The lack of physical growth may come to signify lack of growth in other important areas as well. Dwyer and Mayer (1968) conclude that the reason that being different in adolescence is so difficult is because being different is tantamount to being inferior, and to be short is to be thought of as especially inferior.

Siegel (1982), writing in the *Handbook of Developmental Psychology*, reminds the reader that physical size, appearance, and abilities are standards by which people evaluate themselves and others beginning in early childhood. With the onset of puberty, the concerns about bodily appearance come to the forefront. He adds that:

> Even among normal children, approximately one-third of the adolescent boys report distress and dissatisfaction with some aspect of their physical development or appearance (p. 539).

Jones (1957) followed the later career of boys who were early or late maturers. In this study, the California Psychological Inventory and the Edwards Personal Preference Schedule were administered, and a number of significant differences between the two groups were found. The early maturers scored higher on measures of "good impression and socialization" (p. 127). Where differences had been ascertained in adolescence, they remained in adulthood. Mussen and Jones (1957) concluded that the difference between early and late maturers with respect to adolescent personality attributes including motivation, self-concepts, and attitudes toward others were rather durable over time. It should be noted, however, that there is also some evidence that late maturers, especially those with strong intellectual capabilities from middle-class backgrounds, may be relatively flexible, adaptable, and successful in their adult years (Mussen 1962). It would be interesting to investigate if that subgroup of late maturers who eventually caught up to their peers in height—or actually grew to above-average stature—were more likely to achieve a successful adult adjustment than those who remained very short.

Ames (1957) also reported long-term disadvantages associated with late maturing. She analyzed data from a longitudinal study and found that adult social behavior was correlated with level of physical maturation during adolescence. The participants were forty men who were members of the Adolescent Growth Study at the University of California, Berkeley. Adult social behavior was partitioned into "informal social participation, formal social participation, and occupational participation." The results of this study paralleled previous findings that the psychological, physical, and social advantages for early maturers are maintained into adulthood. The late maturers, on the other hand, were found to either remain or become less socially active as a group as they got older.

In Ames' (1957) investigation, the rate of maturation during adolescence as measured by skeletal age indexes determined from x-rays proved to be a better predictor of adult social behavior than any of the other variables used. Just this one factor, relating to physical stature, was the most reliable predictor of adult social behavior. In fact, if the one percent level of confidence had been used as a test of the null hypothesis, only this index of skeletal maturation would have proven significantly related to individual differences in adult social behavior.

Siegel (1982) notes that "the short, beardless, and generally immature boy will suffer social and psychological consequences." The short, physically mature youngster, though experiencing difficulties, is generally not at as much of a disadvantage as the short, physically immature child. In any case, however, it is a confusing world for the smaller than average male because:

> A contrasting set of expectations entirely faces those growing up small. What's "expected" of them is childlike behavior. Looking younger than they are because of their size, such children get treated as younger even by bigger kids their own age (Keyes 1980, p. 279).

Human beings have an automatic, unthinking capacity to orient themselves toward other people on the basis of stature and physique as indexes of age and mental maturity. Short stature is clearly associated with a perception that such men are immature and weak. Being a very short male is the type of constitutionally based characteristic that is related to a higher risk of maltreatment by both family members and peers (Biller and Solomon 1986).

In summary, compared to early maturers, late maturers have been found to be consistently less well-adjusted, with poorer social and behavioral skills. Such data indicate that the potentially powerful impact of physical size on personality development has been underestimated. This is particularly the case for the short, immature-looking male.

> Since growth is considered an important achievement, children are proud of surpassing others and of approaching or even—in adolescence—exceeding the height of their parents. If we further add the power tallness gives and the disadvantages shortness holds for children and adolescents in the group of their contemporaries, the significance of height in the competition between the sexes, the equating of tallness with adulthood and shortness with the subordinate estate of childhood, we can understand the desirability and "beauty" of tallness (Beigel 1954, p. 257).

Heterosexual Relationships

Data supporting the hypothesis that short men are not viewed as being as attractive as tall men is overwhelming. This awareness emerges rather forcefully for the short male as he approaches adolescence if he has not already realized it at an earlier age. Quite simply, the shorter male is not as desirable a dating partner (Graziano et al. 1978) and "shorter males, as a rule, do not strike the female as true men" (Beigel 1954, p. 268). At the very least, it is clear that the short boy is socially handicapped (Dwyer and Mayer 1968). The short male develops in a social context in which fewer positive options are available to him. The short boy intuitively knows, and his peers frequently emphasize, the social reality that: "Personality and all other things being equal, most girls probably prefer tall and handsome boys to those who are short and handsome" (Dwyer and Mayer 1968, p. 366).

Even when the short boy is good-looking he is found wanting in terms of an essential male ingredient: height. This is bound to have some developmental implications. Even those individuals of short stature who go on to become high achievers often bitterly recount their developmental difficulties. For example, the highly successful actor Dudley Moore, in recounting his past, said:

> I felt very humiliated about my height when I was a child. Then, when I became interested in what can only be described as the opposite sex, I felt that being small was a disadvantage. I felt unworthy of anything, a little runt (Moore 1983, p. 70).

The universally acknowledged cardinal rule of dating and mate selection is that the male will be significantly taller than his female partner. This rule is almost inviolable (Gillis 1982, Graziano et al. 1978). In fact, Keyes (1980) conducted a survey in which he found that out of seventy-nine women, only two (both were 5'11") said they would date a man shorter than themselves. The remainder of the women reported that, on the average, they would only date a man who was at least 1.7 inches taller than themselves.

In a study examining the influence of the male's height on interpersonal attraction, Graziano et al. (1978) found a profound impact. In this research 100 short, average, and tall women, ages eighteen to twenty-two, evaluated pictures of men whom they believed to be either short, average, or tall. All women, regardless of their own height, found tall men to be significantly more attractive than short men. Men of "average" height (defined as almost six feet tall in this study) were perceived as being the most attractive and well-liked, and as having the most desirable personality traits.

The notion that a relationship exists between height and marital choice is a long-standing one. More than eighty years ago, Pearson and Lee (1903) concluded from their research that there was strong evidence that stature was a major factor in mate selection. Beigel (1954) found that for almost all the couples he studied, the men were taller than the women. Beigel also asked young adults to describe the characteristics of a desirable mate. When interviewing women, he found that "an unexpected number of replies referred to body height" (p. 258) as one of the most important physical characteristics in considering a man as attractive.

Gillis and Avis (1980) investigated the male-taller norm as it applied to mate selection. They examined the height recorded on bank account applications for married couples and discovered that the chances of the male being shorter than the female spouse was 1 in 720. This finding was far less than the statistical expectancy of 3.4 per hundred. The stricture regarding the man being taller than the woman as a basic foundation of perceived physical attractiveness is so prevalent as to be totally taken for granted. The short male's relationships with women are profoundly affected by his stature. "No adult is more painfully aware of who's bigger than a smaller man competing with a larger one for the attention of a woman" (Keyes 1980, p. 147).

The influence of height in human relationships is not limited to interactions between men and women. Berkowitz (1969) studied the friendship choices of undergraduate male subjects. The subjects listed their own heights and then the perceived heights of their three closest friends. Among the friends that he studied, the average difference between the two parties was only 2.76 inches. This reflects a smaller difference than would have occurred in a random pairing of the subjects and suggests that men do not feel comfortable being friendly with peers who are much shorter (or taller) than themselves.

Whether or not one is physically attractive is important in many areas of human endeavor. People make assumptions regarding an individual's behavior and personality traits based on the individual's appearance. It is quite evident that short men are not viewed as being as attractive as taller men and that they may have restricted dating, marital, and friendship choices. The short male is often the recipient of negatively valenced stereotypes, and he is the target of social discrimination which may be based exclusively on the fact that he is significantly shorter than his male peers. Although the complexity of the relationship between height and attractiveness is not fully understood, it is a phenomenon that clearly exists.

4
The Social Context

To understand the developmental significance of short stature, it is imperative to view it in interaction with social influences and the social comparison process.

Meyerson (1963), in writing about physical disability, said: "It is clear that the handicap is not in the body nor in the person, but is a function of the society in which the person lives" (p. 13). It is an essential fact of life that the way an individual feels about his height largely depends on his height relative to others. "Asked if he was self-conscious about his height, the 5'6" Dick Cavett replied: 'No, but I'm self-conscious about other people's'" (Keyes 1980, p. 12).

Consciousness about relative height applies to tall as well as to short individuals. For example, "Thomas Wolfe, the 6'6" writer, used to say that he never felt tall when alone in his apartment; only when he stepped outside was he reminded (incessantly) by others of how big he was relative to them" (Keyes 1980, p. 51).

Within the social context an individual learns that his body is different. In fact, he may experience his own height differently depending on whom he is standing next to. Fisher (1973) makes the point that:

> We only judge our bodies in a most relative way. We have all had the experience of feeling altered in body size as the result of interacting with someone with unusual body dimensions or special significance to us. If you stand next to a very short person, you will feel tall, and in the presence of another who is of extreme height, you suddenly become conscious of your smallness (p. 11).

Ziller (1973) notes that the individual has recourse to "paired-comparisons" of the self and significant others. "That is, self-evaluation evolves in terms of social reality. Self-evaluation then emerges within a social frame of reference" (p. 84). This is a most critical point in the understanding of the psychosocial implications of short stature in males.

One of the first researchers to address specifically the issue of the social comparison process in the development of body image was Schilder (1935) in his book *The Image and Appearance of the Human Body*. In his discussion about body image he states that: "Our body is not isolated. A body is necessarily a body among other bodies. We must have others about us. There is no sense in the word 'ego' when there is not an 'other'" (p. 281).

In a later work, Schilder (1951) reinforces this point by defining the I-Thou relationship more sharply.

> We experience the body image of others. Experience of our body image and experience of the bodies of others are closely interwoven with each other. Just as our emotions and actions are inseparable from the body image, the emotions and actions of others are inseparable from their bodies (p. 16).

According to the psychoanalytic perspective of Schilder (1951), an individual invests his body with libidinous energy. The interest that others show in an individual's body contributes to the manner in which this libidinous drive is developed and then cathected. That is, how attractive we feel depends, to a large extent, on how attractive others think we are. Schilder (1951) emphasizes that others may show their interest in us by actions, words, or attitudes that convey a relationship and a relative valuation between their bodies and our bodies.

If an individual learns that he has a defective body, the social context in which he exists may be extremely upsetting to him. As Fisher (1973) writes:

> The distress stirred up in someone who feels he has a defective body when he finds himself interacting with a person whose body he perceives as not being defective (and therefore presumably superior to his) is profound indeed (p. 82).

Fisher (1973) believes that the individual who perceives his own body to be defective will experience the presence of a sound body as a "reproach to his inferior state, and he becomes disturbed" (p. 82). Just such a process is what the short male may experience throughout his life cycle.

Body Stereotyping

The basis of a relationship between an individual's physical attributes and his personality and behavior may, in part, be a function of the phenomenon of body stereotyping. Over thirty years ago Brodsky (1954) demonstrated that stereotypes exist within our culture regarding the personality traits expected of individuals with different physiques. There are, indeed, very pronounced opinions within all subcultures regarding the supposed association between body characteristics and personality (Lerner 1969, Lerner and Korn 1972, Staffieri 1967). Available research evidence generally supports the hypothesis that a relationship exists between body stereotyping and personality functioning (e.g., Dion, Berscheid, and Walster 1972; Gascaly and Borges 1979; Wallace 1941; Yates and Taylor 1978).

Beliefs regarding the relationship between body characteristics and personality traits are absorbed early in the child's development. Staffieri (1967) asked male children between the ages of six and ten to assign adjectives of various behavior and personality traits to silhouettes which represented extreme endomorphic, mesomorphic, and ectomorphic body types. The results clearly demonstrated that common stereotypes associating personality and behavior traits with various body types existed even at this early age. The significant adjectives assigned to the mesomorph were favorable and related to social assertiveness, while the adjectives assigned to the endomorph and ectomorph were unfavorable and emphasized socially submissive behavior. Moreover, the subjects showed a clear preference to look like the mesomorphic image. The results point to the fact that the concept of the ideal masculine body type is internalized well before adolescence.

Even among young children, there is also a definite link between body type and behavior. Biller (1968) noted that, according to teacher ratings, kindergarten boys who were tall and broad tended to be particularly masculine in interpersonal situations. In a very extensive series of studies with nursery-school-age children, Walker (1962, 1963) clearly demonstrated that among both boys and girls, those with a mesomorphic body type were particularly assertive, socially active, and dominant in peer group activities. Endomorphic and ectomorphic children were generally at a disadvantage when compared to mesomorphic children. Adults, including parents and teachers, consistently rated the actual behavior of mesomorphic children as more positive than that of children with a non-mesomorphic body type. Biller's (1968) results also indicate that height, in itself, actually relates to the social behavior of young boys, with tall boys typically being much more socially influential and dominant than short boys. Boys of average height also surpassed short boys with respect to masculine behavior in social situations. The most clear-cut differences occurred when tall mesomorphic boys were compared to those who were short and had a non-mesomorphic body type. Among preschool children, other evidence shows that tall boys are more popular with their male peers than short boys (Eisenberg et al. 1984).

Lerner and Korn (1972) evaluated three age groups of males (five to six years old, fourteen to fifteen years old, and nineteen to twenty years old) in a study of body stereotype development. It was found that all three age groups held a much more favorable view of the mesomorph than of either the ectomorph or endomorph. Yates and Taylor (1978) investigated young adults' knowledge about and preference for the three primary body types. Their findings confirmed that people clearly associate positive personality characteristics with a mesomorphic body type and would prefer this body type for themselves, while viewing ectomorphic and endomorphic body types as more often connected to negative personality characteristics and as less desirable. Yates and Taylor's data underscored the existence of a general cultural preference for the mesomorphic body type and are consistent with the notion that somatotype-personality correlations are due to stereotyping. There is strong evidence that socially desirable personality traits tend to be attributed to those with a particular body type. Those who are seen as being physically attractive are more likely to be viewed as having more desirable personality traits than those who are labeled as physically unattractive (Dion, Berscheid, and Walster 1972).

In general, being a tall man is strongly associated with being considered by others to be physically attractive and to possess positive personality character-istics. Wallace (1941) instructed college students to make judgments about people they didn't know on the basis of examining their photographs. He found that taller individuals were rated as possessing more positive qualities and were often perceived as good-looking and likable. These findings were confirmed in another study of the relationship between physical characteristics and the perception of masculine traits (Elman 1977). Under the guise of being asked to judge an essay submitted to a writing contest, college students made trait ratings of the con-testants. The students were given information from a contest application form, on which the target person's (i.e., the essay writer's) height was given as either 5'4" or 6'4". Subjects rated the tall contestant as more extroverted and more attractive than they did the short contestant even though the only difference between them was the height listed on the application form.

In an especially interesting investigation, Gascaly and Borges (1979) at-tempted to analyze the interactive effect of height and other body type variables on the attribution of personality characteristics. They asked undergraduates to match personality traits to male body types which varied by height (tall or short). The mesomorphic body type was generally associated with more socially desir-able personality traits than any other body type, but it was also found that "the added dimension of height provided sufficient differentiation of body type to alter significantly behavioral expectancies" (p. 97). The height variable further exaggerated the characteristics generally attributed to different body types. The tall mesomorphic figures were rated in especially positive terms while the short endomorphic and short ectomorphic figures were the recipients of very negative characteristics.

Discussing the developmental implications of their findings, Gascaly and Borges (1979) stated that:

> Since an individual's physique is generally quite stable, it seems reasonable to assume that these stereotypic attributes associated with height (X) body-build combinations are communicated to the individual in terms of both expected behaviors and societal pressure to conform to its beliefs. If over a lifetime, an individual gradually succumbs to these societal expectations, the stereotype is perpetuated. Additionally, the male whose body type does not conform to the traditional image of the ideal male, that of the tall mesomorph, may face severe difficulty in accepting himself and having others accept him as truly masculine and competent in the male role (p. 101).

Women as well as men share similar values about stereotyping the relationship between body type and personality in males. Martel and Biller (1987) found that college-age females possess strong and consistently negative attitudes about short men. In an earlier study aimed at assessing stereotypes concerning the relationship between body type and personality, Lerner (1969) found that females of various ages (late adolescent, adult, middle-aged) hold a common stereotype of that relationship. Females consistently favored the large mesomorphic male in comparison to males with other body types. Lerner's findings strongly supported the social inculcation hypothesis which states that individuals in the child's socializing environment stereotypically associate various behavior and personality traits with specific body types and this association is communicated in subtle yet powerful and long-lasting ways. Eisenberg et al. (1984) provided evidence that mothers of preschool children rate tall boys as more competent than small boys even when the children are the same age.

However, the notion of the superiority of a particular body type for males is not just a social invention. According to cross-cultural evidence, a mesomorphic body type is preferred for males in all societies (Ford and Beach 1951). Similarly, although average height may vary from society to society, it is clear that being relatively tall is also advantageous in all known cultures. It is interesting to note that being heavy seems to be valued in some third world and economically underdeveloped countries because it is seen as being connected to relative affluence. In poorer societies, where many people suffer from the insufficient availability of food and proper nutrition, those who have a more ample supply and are bigger are valued (and envied) for their success. There is inconsistent cross-cultural agreement about the ideal body type for women. Expectations about ideal body types for women also vary more across different historical epochs in a particular society as well as between societies. Some cultures emphasize petiteness, while others emphasize females being heavier than current U.S. standards. Again, in some underdeveloped countries the heavy woman may be a symbol of relative leisure and economic success (Seward 1946).

Social Power

Males in our society, whether tall or short, often seem obsessed with the significance of their relative height and how it may affect their influence with other people.

> Duke was six-four, but he wore four inch lifts and a ten-gallon hat. He had a station wagon modified to fit all that paraphernalia. He even had the overheads raised on his boats so that he would walk through the doorways with the lifts on. And he was bigger than them all (Mitchum 1983, p. 52).

> We short people think we're of average height and people taller than us above average, says 5′5″ physician George Shorago of South San Francisco Hospital.

He adds, "In medical school I sometimes had to stand on a stool when I operated. It was tough on me until I became chief resident. Then everybody had to bend down to accommodate me" (*U.S. News and World Report*, March 28, 1977, p. 63).

As Korda (1975) reminds us in his book on power, height is something that we need to be constantly aware of in our day-to-day dealings with others. We exist in a social context in which an individual's body is judged in comparison with other bodies. Keyes (1980) postulates that height is seen in relative terms, by level of eye contact, and in equation with power. All three of these components are germane to understanding the psychology of the short male. Fisher (1970) has pointed out that a "primitive evaluation" process goes on between individuals that may be based solely on height. Biologist Stephen Jay Gould states that, among both men and animals, "gaze behavior" is an important means of sorting out who stands where. "In essence, it is important whether you are looking up or looking down" (cited in Keyes 1980, p. 52). This perspective translates into greater or lesser social power.

A workable definition of social power is offered by Caplan and Goldman (1981): "Social power is the ability to move others spatially or otherwise and to induce others to defer to one's wishes" (p. 171). There is research to suggest that short males have considerably less social power than their taller counterparts. As emphasized earlier in this book, individuals thought to be more important are judged to be taller. There seems to be a natural tendency to associate power with larger size. As Keyes (1980) points out:

> It is a basic tenet of the psychology of perception that size is associated with value. Whatever our mind judges as important our eye will judge large. And power is among our ultimate values (p. 57).

In one of the earliest research efforts addressing this supposition a half-century ago, Eisenberg (1937) wrote that physical factors "such as height and weight play some role in determining a boy's dominance and status among his fellows" (p. 90). At that time the quantitative influence of such factors could not be ascertained.

The role of height in determining dominance and status is so important that it has been mentioned as one of the rules for choosing a vice-presidential candidate of the United States. ABC news correspondent Roger Mudd reported: "Rule number three: go short, pick a vice president shorter than you are. If you can't do that, make sure to stand at least ten feet away from him" (Mudd, 1984).

Fisher (1973) predicted that an individual who regards his body or parts of it as inferior will be particularly vulnerable to a sense of intimidation. Individuals who feel threatened because of physical inferiority will develop defensive styles and attempt to create environments that they will experience as safe. As discussed in chapter 3, such defensive styles may endure because of the difficulty the short male has in negotiating situations in which the power dimension is prevalent.

Hartnett, Bailey, and Hartley (1974) examined the hypothesis that body height determines the amount of personal space given to an individual. Within an experimental situation, they had male and female subjects approach either a tall or a short person with instructions to stop when they felt uncomfortable. Their findings revealed that the subjects stopped their approaches further from the tall person than from the short person.

> Both males and females maintain twice as much distance between themselves and the tall object person. This is most apparent in the standing position where the mean space for subjects were 9.8 inches and 22.7 inches for the short and tall subjects respectively (p. 134).

Height is clearly a major factor in the amount of personal space accorded an individual.

Bailey (1976) studied the relationship between body size and implied threat. He found that subjects consistently rated larger people as more potentially threatening and intimidating than they did smaller people. The powerful perceptual impact of the large person was strikingly apparent from the data. Bailey also found that the greatest perceptual differences for large person versus small person occurred under the strongest threat condition. He concluded that: "For whatever reasons, it seems clear that physical size and being 'smaller than' or 'larger than' played major roles in the subject-object interactions in the present study" (p. 228). As Keyes (1980) postulated, height is seen within a relative social context and is a major factor in determining relative power. It is, perhaps, the element of the primitive evaluation which is operating, albeit on a less than fully conscious level of awareness (Fisher 1970).

Caplan and Goldman's (1981) data confirmed two predictions regarding the relationship between height and social power: When given a choice between violating a tall or short person's space, subjects intrude more often into the short person's space. In comparison to males, females who are given a choice of violating the space of a tall or a short person are less likely to invade the space of the tall person. Summarizing their findings, Caplan and Goldman concluded that: "The present study, by using an experimental situation which contained a relatively small degree of threat provided evidence that height alone is a sufficiently robust characteristic to affect interpersonal spacing" (p. 170).

The amount of social power an individual enjoys is dependent, at least in part, upon his height. Size and power within Western culture appear to be related almost linearly. Fisher (1973) succinctly articulates the social power dynamic as it relates to the function of height: "If someone is unmistakably shorter than average, almost everyone has the right to feel bigger and to entertain a sense of superiority by laughing 'down'" (p. 189).

Status

Power and ascribed status go hand in glove. It has also been hypothesized that height and ascribed status are positively correlated. The research overwhelmingly supports the notion that height is associated with status and that people tend to assume that individuals of higher status are also taller. More than sixty-five years ago, Thorndike (1920) pointed out that taller individuals benefit from the "halo effect," that is, others will attribute positive personality characteristics to them. Gillis (1982) describes this situation as: "a problem, a problem of prejudice, if what they think of us depends on how tall we are. That, unfortunately, is what the research literature shows" (p. 61).

Dannenmaier and Thumin (1964) studied whether perceptual judgements of height would be influenced by the authority status of the person being evaluated. They hypothesized a linear relationship between status and perceived height. Their subjects were female nursing students who had four individuals of different authority levels represented to them: an assistant director of nursing, a course instructor, a class president, and a fellow student. The results confirmed the hypothesis: There was an overestimation of the authority figure's height and an underestimation of the student's height.

The Dannenmaier and Thumin (1964) study, while an important contribution, did not rule out a competing hypothesis put forward by Wilson (1968). According to Wilson, "the systematic overestimation and underestimation could be related not to status but to general body somatotypes, facial characteristics, personality attributes, or to numerous unknown and uncontrolled for aspects of the authority figures used" (p. 97). To correct this bias, only a single stimulus figure, who was unknown to the subjects, was used. By doing this, it was hypothesized that an increase in status would be related to a tendency to increase the height estimates for the stimulus figure. Five groups of students had the stimulus figure's academic status described at five different levels. As in Dannenmaier and Thumin's (1964) study, the subjects increased their estimates of the individual's height in direct proportion to the level of his ascribed academic status.

All in all, the research solidly demonstrates that height is a very important factor in perceived power and social status. The taller individual is able to attain a more commanding position in the eyes of others, benefiting from the positive attributions based on his height. Once again, the definition of the socially powerful individual is: One who has the ability to move others spatially or otherwise and to induce others to defer to one's wishes (Caplan and Goldman 1981, p. 171).

The psychosocial and developmental implications of short stature in males become clear. The short male compared to the tall male is generally the recipient of attributions relating to less competence, power, heterosexual attractiveness, and status.

Another question that might be broached relates to whether there is, in reality, any connection between height and intellectual competence. Overall, there does indeed seem to be a slightly positive correlation between height and intelligence. This correlation is due to factors which are not, in reality, very relevant for the great majority of individuals. One reason for the correlation is that individuals with biological handicaps that affect their growth are *sometimes* retarded, or handicapped to some extent in their cognitive functioning. Interestingly, a study of preschool children by Eisenberg et al. (1984) found a positive relationship between boys' height and their competence in Piagetian correspondence and conservation tasks.

Among the relatively small proportion of our population that is retarded, those who are severely or profoundly retarded are also likely to suffer from very short stature. Of course, there are some cases where extremely severe parental deprivation and maltreatment may contribute to both intellectual and physical growth deficiencies. On the other hand, there is a slight overall correlation between intelligence and height because individuals who have higher socioeconomic status tend to benefit from better nutrition and medical care than do those with lower socioeconomic status. Poor prenatal care among the poor may be a factor contributing to the lowering of both intellectual and stature potential (Biller and Solomon 1986).

Although the correlation between height and intelligence is statistically significant for large heterogeneous populations, it generally does not have any practical significance: You certainly can't judge a person's intelligence by his height. But again, the halo effect associated with height may, indeed, lead many people to expect that tall men are brighter than short men. Prospective employers, for example, may subtly overrate the tall man's intellectual competence while underestimating that of the short man.

Vocational Discrimination

The most frequent question I'm asked is, "How do I get promoted?" My answer: "The easiest way is to be born right and born tall." (Gerard Roche, President, Heidrick and Struggles, Inc., *American Way*, January 1978, p. 49.)

The placement director for a big midwestern university overheard one corporate recruiter say to another "I wonder if so-and-so's ready for management? He's only five-foot-four." ("Short People—Are They Being Discriminated Against?" *U.S. News and World Report*, March 28, 1977, p. 68.)

Why is it that a space for your height is in third or fourth position on every application blank in the world? What difference does it make in getting into medical school or going to work for a corporation? ("Short Workers of the World Unite!" Deck, L., *Psychology Today*, 1971, p. 102.)

The literature reviewed so far makes it clear that "there is a pervasive social attitude which associates tallness with positive psychological characteristics and assigns negative attributes to shortness" (Stabler et al. 1980, p. 743). Discrimination against short males, although often subtle, remains a powerful factor in their lives. As pointed out in a previous section of this chapter, discrimination against males of short stature begins in early childhood. Society positively frames an identity for the short female by labeling her as "cute" or "dainty," while the short boy is just plain short (Finch 1978). This discriminatory posture makes its way into all important life spheres.

Taller individuals are routinely favored in both social and economic endeavors, although there is little public acknowledgement of this fact (Keyes 1980). In the economic realm, for example, shorter men not only receive lower salaries, but they are also less likely to be hired in the first place in spite of otherwise equal qualifications (Graziano et al. 1978). In a survey at the University of Pittsburgh, graduating seniors who were 6′2″ or taller received a starting salary 12.4 percent higher than graduates who were under six feet (Deck 1971). In a study conducted by Kurtz (1969), recruiters were asked to make a hypothetical hiring decision between two equally qualified candidates who differed in height. The height bias in favor of the taller candidate was dramatically evident. Seventy-two percent of the recruiters said that they would hire the taller candidate.

John Kenneth Galbraith articulately described the favored treatment of taller individuals as "one of the most blatant and forgiven prejudices in our society" (*The Christian Science Monitor*, May 18, 1977, p. 22). In this interview, he describes a conversation that he'd had with General Charles de Gaulle about their shared attitude regarding the advantages of being very tall. Galbraith in a somewhat facetious, but basically serious, manner stated: "We tall men, being higher than anybody else, are much more visible and thus more closely watched. Therefore, it follows that our behavior is naturally superior. So the world instinctively and rightly trusts tall men" (p. 22).

Discrimination against the short male is most often more subtle than Galbraith's statement would indicate. In fact, the discrimination is more often what Keyes (1980) calls "like fighting a ghost." The reason for this is twofold: Either the awareness regarding discrimination is not in the consciousness of one or both individuals in a particular social situation, or verbalization of the discrimination is suppressed. The result is that the short male feels that something is subtly awry, but he cannot pin it down. He may believe that this discrimination is based on the social feedback that he does not look quite right, that he falls significantly short of the cultural ideal for height. Yet, according to the prevailing advertised American ideology that we are all basically created equal, that performance and competence are what counts, appearance is ostensibly relatively unimportant. Needless to say, at this point, appearance often seems to transcend (or obscure) other qualities in the process of social judgement, particularly where first impressions are involved. A person's salient physical characteristics, of which height is one, do, in fact, exert a powerful influence both on the way others perceive him and on the way he thinks and feels about himself.

There are, of course, quite formalized types of discrimination against short individuals, as when an explicit criterion for minimal stature is set on the assumption that those below a certain height do not have the physical competence and/or social influence necessary to do the job. Traditionally, for example, positions in police and fire departments have been closed to individuals with short stature (typically defined as less than 5'7" or 5'8"). Fortunately, there has been much legal pressure to develop more competency-based standards that will not automatically exclude those with short stature; height requirements have especially discriminated against men from lower-socioeconomic minority backgrounds and women (Hogan and Quigley 1986).

Summary

Males are particularly concerned about body characteristics associated with size, strength, and overall perceptual impact. Males strongly desire and strive for the attainment of the 6'2" cultural ideal. The research confirms the belief that large body size in males is associated with positive body cathexis. There is a very strong linear relationship between a male's satisfaction with his height and its closeness to the cultural ideal. Males do, indeed, value bigness of body parts, and the large, mesomorphic build symbolizes masculinity within Western culture. A male's sense of self and masculinity is, to a large degree, interwoven with the concept of bigness.

Research addressing the question of self-concept and body cathexis indicates that an individual's negative feelings about his body are associated with feelings of insecurity involving his self. The way an individual feels about his body has a substantial effect on the way he feels about his total self. Equally as important in this complex equation is the point that the way other people feel about an individual's body can greatly influence his own perceptions of self-worth and self-esteem.

While there has not been much literature directly assessing the developmental implications of short stature in males, more has been written concerning the impact of early versus late maturation. Among males, short stature has been found to be correlated with late maturation, and late maturers have been found to be consistently less well-adjusted, and to have poorer social and behavioral skills when compared to early maturers.

A relationship exists between large physical size and positively valued behavioral traits. Intensely pejorative stereotypes are associated with shortness and nonmesomorphic body types which are absorbed even by very young children. The short male learns to perceive his own body as defective, and the social milieu reinforces his sense of inadequacy. Lerner's (1969) social inculcation model seems a parsimonious but oversimplified explanation of the phenomenon.

Short stature in males may lead to a characteristic defensive style. This style may take the form of excessive reliance on rational and analytical skills with a parallel devaluation of the body world. In order to satisfy the need to express anger and aggressive impulses without the fear of retribution, the short male often develops a well-differentiated sense of humor. This characteristic style may also serve as a means of gaining peer group acceptance, that is, while not being able to compete on an equal physical basis (or at least believing that he cannot do so), the short male may be admitted to the peer group because of his better-than-average cognitive skills, his sense of humor, or his mascot potential. For the short male, this behavior entails acceptance of relatively low social power.

Research solidly demonstrates that greater height is positively related to greater social power and perceived social status. The taller individual is able to attain a more commanding position among others, and he benefits from the positive attributions associated with his height.

It also becomes clear to the short male as he approaches adolescence that he is viewed as less physically attractive. This, in turn, leads to limited dating, marital, and friendship choices. He is the recipient of social discrimination, and this stigmatization spreads to a broader range of situations as he gets older. When the available literature on developmental, personality, and social consequences is viewed as a whole, it is clear that short stature in males can have profound psychosocial implications.

5
Stature, Self-Perceptions, and Stereotypes

This chapter begins with a description of the methodology of a rather extensive project aimed at exploring the linkage between height and psychological functioning. The goals were to focus particularly on the ways in which self-perceptions, self-concept, and body satisfaction might differ among young men as a function of their height. Given previous research (described in chapters 1–4), it was predicted that short men would consistently respond in ways that would produce a patterning of less adequate self-perceptions, including poorer self-concepts and body images, than would men of either average or tall stature. It was also predicted that where differences existed between men of average or tall stature they would favor the latter group. Previous research has indicated that being significantly taller than average for males, other things being equal, is a definite asset in psychological and social development.

This research project differs from previous efforts with respect to the relatively broad range of procedures used to assess various dimensions of psychological and social functioning. Equally important was the effort to assess a group of short males who did not have any potential handicaps other than their relative stature.

Subjects

The subjects were Caucasian males attending college, and were generally from middle-class socioeconomic backgrounds. No doubt sociocultural and ethnic variations exist regarding the ways in which short males behave and are treated by others. However, in order to achieve a sharp focus on the topic and to maximize the internal validity of assessment techniques, a relatively homogenous group of subjects were assessed to minimize the possible confounding of results due to ethnicity and social class. It is interesting to note that the norms for average height have increased over the past several centuries due to improvement in general health and nutritional standards. While the average male was approximately 5'6" when the Pilgrims first arrived in Massachusetts, he is now

5'9". However, according to our best statistical estimates, average height has peaked except for those in the bottom socioeconomic quartile who are generally deprived of the medical and nutritional resources available to the rest of our population (Hetherington and Parke 1986).

Classification on the basis of height can certainly be somewhat arbitrary. The mean height for Caucasian males, eighteen to twenty-four years old, is 5'9". For the purpose of this study, the height groups were as follows: short subjects were between 5'2" and 5'5½", average subjects between 5'8" and 5'10½", and tall subjects between 6' and 6'4". All three of these height category designations were consistent with National Health Survey statistics (Abraham, Johnson, and Najjar 1979; *Statistical Abstract of the United States* 1982).

In order to ensure that categories would be reasonably distinct, data collected on subjects who did not fit into one of the three height categories were not included in the study. Using the above criteria, the subjects whose responses were available for most of the data analyses were distributed in the following way: forty-one were classified as short (mean height 5'4"), thirty-eight as average (mean height 5'9"), and forty as tall (mean height 6'1"). It is important to emphasize that the short group consisted of men who could be categorized as distinctively shorter than average but were not midgets or dwarfs and did not have other specific physical handicaps. Young men between 5'2" and 5'5½" are clearly very short males but can be viewed as being on the normal distribution of height, well within two standard deviations of the norm for men of their age group. On the other hand, men between 5'6" and 5'8" (or even those who are somewhat taller) may be perceived as short (and may view themselves as short), but they seem to be occupants of a rather gray area with respect to relative height. As discussed in chapter 6, issues such as timing of maturation, body type and sociocultural reference group may play an especially important role for men falling into the somewhat below average category.

The subjects were from three universities in the New England area. They ranged in age from seventeen to twenty-two, were primarily unmarried (ninety-four percent), and were generally middle-class (mean family income $30,000). The subjects did not have any health or physically related abnormalities, and the vast majority of those in all three groups reported regular participation in some sport or athletic activity. Students from two introductory psychology courses were asked to volunteer (for extra credit) for a research project dealing with self-perceptions. Students in these classes had the opportunity to choose whether or not to participate in one or more projects conducted each semester, so that they would not feel pressured to volunteer for a particular project. On the cover sheet (read aloud by one of the researchers), subjects were told that the project involved a study of self-concept, but no mention was made of the investigators' interest in height. The research packet given to each subject contained a background questionnaire with items pertaining to age, height, weight, family income, grade point average, and so forth (Martel 1985).

Among the subjects from the two introductory psychology classes, only eighteen short males were available in comparison with thirty-eight average and forty tall subjects. In order to have subject groups of approximately equal size for comparison purposes, it was decided to recruit additional subjects of short stature. This recruitment took place at an ivy league university in New England. An advertisement asking for male volunteers 5'5½" or under was placed in the college newspaper, offering $8.00 for the half-hour commitment to fill out the questionnaire material. In this manner, twenty-three additional short males were included in the research. Whereas there were no significant differences between the different height groups drawn from the state universities, the short subjects recruited from the ivy league school, as a group, had significantly higher family incomes and higher grade point averages than did the other subjects. However, the short subjects from the ivy league school did not significantly differ from the short state university subjects in the means or patterning of their responses to the various assessment techniques (i.e., Body Cathexis Scale, Semantic Differential Measures, Activity Vector Analysis).

Given the purpose of the study to investigate potential self-concept and personality disadvantages associated with short stature, it is noteworthy that the short subjects, as a group, had certain advantages compared to the average and tall groups, that is, more of them came from higher socioeconomic backgrounds and enjoyed a higher educational status because they attended an ivy league school. Other things being equal, such an advantaged status would be expected to be correlated with relatively positive scores on measures of self-concept and to make it less likely that the short subjects would present themselves in a negative light compared to taller subjects. As previously mentioned, however, the short ivy league students responded to the measures in very similar fashion to the short state university students so that they were treated as one group in comparison to average and tall subjects. The implications of these similar response patterns are discussed in chapter 6.

Assessment

The present study utilized five major types of measures. The Body Cathexis Scale (Secord and Jourard 1954) was administered to obtain data concerning how subjects felt about their bodies. The Activity Vector Analysis (Clarke 1956) was utilized to assess self-concept, and a Semantic Differential technique (Osgood, Suci, and Tannenbaum 1957) was designed to determine how positively or negatively a subject felt about men of short, average, and tall height. A structured questionnaire was also developed to gather information pertaining to the perceived importance of height in everyday situations. In addition, in-depth clinical interviews were conducted with some of the short subjects (see chapter 6).

The Body Cathexis Scale

Secord and Jourard (1953) developed the Body Cathexis Scale because they believed that an individual's attitude toward his body is of crucial importance in assessing personality functioning. They postulated that body cathexis is integrally related to self-concept, although identifiable as a separate aspect. The Body Cathexis Scale is designed to measure "the degree of satisfaction or dissatisfaction with the various parts or processes of the body" (Secord and Jourard 1953, p. 343).

The scale was initially developed by asking subjects to indicate the strength and direction of feeling which they have about each of the various parts or functions of the body. The measure was extensively pilot-tested on college students, and items that were difficult to understand or resulted in little variability from subject to subject were eliminated. The results of the Secord and Jourard (1953) study revealed a statistically significant relationship between body cathexis and self-cathexis (r = .58 for men and .66 for women). This supported their hypothesis that the valuation of the body and the self tends to be commensurate. The revised form of the Body Cathexis Scale (Jourard and Secord 1954) was used in the present investigation. The scale consists of forty-one items relating to specific body parts (e.g., hair, hands, nose, waist, legs, chest, and so forth) and bodily processes (e.g., appetite, energy level, digestion, and so forth). For each item, the subjects are asked to indicate on a five-point scale how they feel with regard to themselves (i.e., strong positive feelings, moderately positive feelings, no feelings, moderately negative feelings, or strongly negative feelings).

There are several studies in the literature which have included reliability coefficients for the Body Cathexis Scale. In the earliest of these studies (Secord and Jourard 1953) the split-half reliability coefficient (Spearman-Brown formula) was .78 for male subjects (n = 45) and .83 for female subjects (n = 43). Jourard and Remy (1955) reported a split-half reliability of .91 (n = 99), and Weinberg (1960) found a split-half reliability of .87 (n = 212). There are two reports of test-retest reliability, with the earlier one (Johnson 1956) yielding a reliability coefficient of .72 (six- to eight-week interval) and the latter (Tucker 1981) reporting a reliability coefficient of .87 (two-week interval). Overall, these results suggest that the Body Cathexis Scale is internally consistent and stable over time.

The Activity Vector Analysis

Clarke (1956) developed the Activity Vector Analysis (AVA) to assess various dimensions of self-concept. The scale is constructed in a free-response adjective checklist format, and it is analyzed on both an ipsative and normative basis in order to provide an understanding of the balance and patterns of behavioral tendencies within the individual. The Form E version of the scale was used in this study. This form consists of eighty-seven nonderogatory adjectives that describe human behavior. The AVA allows subjects to respond in a way that is characteristic of their behavior and yields personality descriptions through the measurement of self-concept.

The personality interpretation from the AVA is made through ipsative integration of four basic unipolar factors (i.e., aggressiveness, sociability, emotional stability, and social adaptability). This four-factor model yields 258 specific AVA profiles. The scores obtained, based on factor analytic studies, are compared with scores from the 1,200 subjects used to standardize this version of the instrument.

The AVA system is constructed so that pattern shapes which reflect similar types of self-concepts are spatially close to each other on the universe of all the possible pattern shapes. Hence, similar pattern shapes will form a cluster which is identifiable, that is, those individuals with similar self-concepts will be close together on the pattern universe.

The determination as to whether a particular pattern shape belongs to a cluster is based on a correlation of at least .69 with a pattern shape that has been chosen as the center of the cluster. The pattern shape in the center of the cluster is chosen if it correlates at least .69 with as many of the other pattern shapes as possible. This criterion has been used in previous studies (e.g., Merenda 1964, 1968; Merenda and Mohan 1966; Merenda and Shapurian 1974).

Scoring of the AVA is based on profiles which are generated from the adjectives the subject has checked. These profiles are called "pattern shapes." The pattern shapes are composed of four vectors. Each vector represents the potential for behavior of a specific personality dimension. Vector 1 expresses the degree of *aggressiveness*, vector 2 expresses the degree of *sociability*, vector 3 represents the degree of *emotional stability*, and vector 4 represents the degree of *social adaptability*.

There are several studies in the literature attesting to the construct validity of the AVA (Clarke 1956; Hammer 1958; Musiker 1958; Merenda, Clarke, Musiker, and Kessler 1961). Using four different samples of college subjects, Whisler (1957) found evidence for the descriptive validity of the AVA. Musiker (1958) found that personality variables measured by the AVA can be meaningfully related to scores on the Guilford-Zimmerman Scale. Merenda, Clarke, Musiker, and Kessler (1961) administered both the AVA and Kessler Passive-Dependency Scale to a sample of 99 female and 181 male subjects. The results demonstrated the construct validity for both these instruments.

Several research projects have provided evidence for the reliability of the AVA. In the earliest of these studies by Mosel (1954), the AVA was administered twice within a two-week interval. Reliability estimates of .74 and .73 were obtained for social self-concepts and basic self-concepts, respectively. Merenda and Clarke (1959a) reported profile reliability studies based on five independent samples. With the typical time interval of twelve months, the average reliability coefficients were found to be .77 for image profiles (profiles resulting from a combination of basic self-concept and social self-concept profiles), .75 for social self-concept profiles, and .72 for basic self-concept profiles. In another study of reliability in which a one-month interval was used, test-retest reliability coefficients for social self-concept profiles and basic self-concept profiles were found to be .82 and .78 respectively (Hasler and Clarke 1968).

In the present study, subjects were asked to complete a threefold AVA aimed at assessing their basic self, social self, and ideal self. Subjects were presented with a separate page listing eighty-seven different descriptive adjectives (e.g., decent, sociable, ethical, demanding, funny, tense, impetuous, jovial, pragmatic, tough). On one page they were asked to indicate every adjective that "has ever been used in describing you," on another page they were asked to indicate every adjective that "you honestly believe is descriptive of you," and on a third page, they were asked to indicate every adjective that "you believe describes the ideal person."

The Questionnaire

A questionnaire was specifically prepared for use in the present study (see figure 5-1). The goal was to design a questionnaire that would add a dimension of richness, in the form of both quantitative and qualitative data, regarding the way in which college-age males think and feel about the importance and impact of physical stature.

Literature on questionnaire design was reviewed before constructing the questionnaire for this study (e.g., Best 1977, Moser 1961, Parten 1966). The number of questions was kept to a minimum, and the wording of the questions was simple and easy to understand. The final draft of the questionnaire was pilot-tested on a small group of individuals who were asked to offer suggestions for improving clarity. In order to assess test-retest reliability, this revised question-

---

Using the scale below, please answer the following questions

1–never   4–often
2–rarely   5–always
3–sometimes

1. Do you feel that your height has been a *help* to you socially?   1 2 3 4 5
2. Do you feel that your height has been a *hindrance* to you socially? 1 2 3 4 5
3. Do you ever add inches when reporting your height?   1 2 3 4 5
4. If you could choose any height to be, what would it be?   _ Ft. _ _ In.

The list below contains a number of social situations in which height comparisons might be made. *Using the scale below, indicate to what extent you feel comfortable in each of the situations.*

1–very uncomfortable	4–comfortable
2–somewhat uncomfortable	5–very comfortable
3–neither comfortable nor uncomfortable	

5. Standing in a crowded line	1 2 3 4 5
6. Giving an important presentation in front of a group	1 2 3 4 5
7. On a first date	1 2 3 4 5
8. Involved in a contact sport	1 2 3 4 5
9. At a crowded party	1 2 3 4 5
10. Standing at a club or bar	1 2 3 4 5
11. At an initial business or professional meeting	1 2 3 4 5

Using the scale below, please answer the following questions

1–not important	4–very important
2–slightly important	5–extremely important
3–moderately important	

12. How important do you think a man's height is in acquiring a dating partner? 1 2 3 4 5

13. How important do you think a man's height is in acquiring a marriage partner? 1 2 3 4 5

14. How important do you think a man's height is in terms of being professionally successful in life? 1 2 3 4 5

Using the scale below, please answer the following questions

1–much more than average	4–somewhat less than average
2–somewhat more than average	5–much less than average
3–average	

15. Comparing your physical attractiveness with that of others of your sex and age, how attractive do you think you are? 1 2 3 4 5

16. Comparing your overall desirability as a dating partner with others of your sex and age, how desirable do you think you are? 1 2 3 4 5

17. Comparing your overall desirability as a marriage partner with others of your sex and age, how desirable do you think you are? 1 2 3 4 5

Figure 5–1. Questionnaire Concerning Feelings about Height as It Relates to Social Situations

naire was administered to a group of college-age subjects with a two-week interval between administrations. Test-retest coefficients for individual items ranged from a high of .88 to a low of .38, with an average of .65.

The Semantic Differential Measures

It was decided to construct a semantic differential measure to determine how positively or negatively subjects felt about men who were short, average or tall (see figure 5–2). It was expected that subjects would attribute very different feelings toward men as a function of their height (Martel and Biller 1986).

The Semantic Differential technique was developed as a tool to study the psychology of meaning (Osgood, Suci, and Tannenbaum 1957). Although the Semantic Differential technique is often referred to as if it were some kind of test having some definite set of items, this is not the case. On the contrary, "it is a very general way of getting at a certain type of information; a highly generalizable technique of measurement which must be adapted to the requirement of each research problem to which it is applied" (Osgood, Suci, and Tannenbaum 1957, p. 77).

The usefulness of the Semantic Differential technique is evident in its successful application in many different contexts. It has been used in research on such varied problems as clinical diagnoses, vocational choices, cultural differences, and consumers' reactions to products and brand names (Snider and Osgood 1969).

Osgood, Suci, and Tannenbaum (1957), using a factor analytic technique, found that three major factors accounted for the largest percentage of total variance. In the order of amount of variance accounted for, they are Evaluation, Potency, and Activity. *Evaluation* is interpreted as "goodness," *potency* is interpreted as "strength," and *activity* is interpreted as expressing "motion or action." Osgood, Suci, and Tannenbaum (1957) reported a test-retest reliability coefficient of .85 in a study having 100 subjects complete ratings on 40 different scales.

The adjectives used in the construction of the Semantic Differential for the present study were culled from several sources (Albaum, Best, and Hawkins 1981; Coyne and Holzman 1966; Harigopal 1979; Osgood, Suci, and Tannenbaum 1957).

For the purpose of assessing the internal consistency of the Semantic Differential measures used in the present study, a coefficient alpha (Cronbach 1951) was computed for each of the following concepts: men of short height, men of average height, and men of tall height. The results of these analyses reveal a rather high level of internal consistency, with all three scales yielding alpha coefficients in the mideighties (i.e., men of short height, .84; men of average height, .85; men of tall height, .87). To assure that the measures were stable over time, a test-retest reliability assessment was conducted. Using eighty-two subjects, the measures were administered twice with a two-week interval. The test-retest re-

Instructions

On this page you will find a concept to be judged and beneath it is a set of seventeen paired items. Circle the number on each of the seventeen paired items that best reflects your feeling about the concept listed at the top of the page. Be sure to circle only one number on each set of paired items.

Men of Short Height

Mature	1 2 3 4 5 6 7	Immature —
Inhibited	1 2 3 4 5 6 7	Uninhibited —
Bad	1 2 3 4 5 6 7	Good —
Positive	1 2 3 4 5 6 7	Negative —
Secure	1 2 3 4 5 6 7	Insecure —
Conforming	1 2 3 4 5 6 7	Individualistic —
Feminine	1 2 3 4 5 6 7	Masculine —
Active	1 2 3 4 5 6 7	Passive —
Incomplete	1 2 3 4 5 6 7	Complete —
Successful	1 2 3 4 5 6 7	Unsuccessful —
Optimistic	1 2 3 4 5 6 7	Pessimistic —
Dirty	1 2 3 4 5 6 7	Clean —
Dominant	1 2 3 4 5 6 7	Submissive —
Outgoing	1 2 3 4 5 6 7	Withdrawn —
Aggressive	1 2 3 4 5 6 7	Timid —
Not capable	1 2 3 4 5 6 7	Capable —
Confident	1 2 3 4 5 6 7	Not Confident —

Figure 5–2. Semantic Differential Measure Concerning Men of Short Height

liability for men of short height was .81; men of average height, .64; and men of tall height, .72.

The results are presented in the following order: questionnaire data, Body Cathexis Scale, Semantic Differential findings, Activity Vector Analysis, and women's perceptions. Data from the in-depth clinical interviews with short men are presented in chapter 6.

Questionnaire Data

Each item of the questionnaire was subjected to an analysis of variance (ANOVA) among the three height groups (short, average, tall). The assumption for homogeneity of variance was tested, and none of the groups were found to be heterogeneous. If significant ANOVA results were achieved, a Tukey (HSD) Test was used as a follow-up procedure in order to ascertain the specific significant differences (Winer 1971). The results of the ANOVA and Tukey analyses may be found in tables 5-1, 5-2 and 5-3.

> *Question 1:* Do you feel that your height has been a help to you socially?
>
> *Question 2:* Do you feel that your height has been a hindrance to you socially?

Questions 1 and 2 were designed to assess whether subjects thought that the dimension of height has a social advantage or disadvantage.

Table 5–1
Questionnaire Responses: Means and Standard Deviations for Short, Average, and Tall Men

Question Number[a]	Grand Mean	Number	Short		Average		Tall	
			Mean	Standard Deviation	Mean	Standard Deviation	Mean	Standard Deviation
1	2.57	119	2.12	0.86	2.38	0.89	3.22	0.95
2	2.04	120	3.24	0.82	1.53	0.80	1.28	0.45
3	1.58	120	1.79	1.14	1.61	0.89	1.35	0.77
5	2.92	119	2.68	0.99	2.82	1.04	3.25	1.17
6	2.92	120	3.14	1.26	3.08	1.05	2.55	1.32
7	2.79	120	2.31	0.87	3.00	1.04	3.10	1.13
8	3.52	120	3.12	1.21	3.39	1.03	4.05	0.96
9	3.19	119	2.58	0.95	3.18	1.06	3.82	0.98
10	3.13	120	2.57	0.98	3.21	1.04	3.65	0.98
11	3.17	120	2.93	0.78	3.29	0.80	3.30	1.02
12	2.75	120	3.19	0.83	2.58	0.98	2.45	1.13
13	2.14	120	2.19	1.02	2.32	1.14	1.93	1.10
14	2.33	120	2.24	1.00	2.47	1.22	2.30	1.04
15	2.63	120	2.93	0.84	2.50	0.65	2.45	0.75
16	2.50	120	2.71	1.04	2.42	0.64	2.38	0.84
17	2.35	119	2.19	0.89	2.57	0.84	2.33	0.94

[a]For Question 4, see figure 5-3.

Table 5–2
ANOVA Tests for the Questionnaire Data

Question	Source	SS	df	MS	F	p
1	Height Group	27.06	2	13.53	16.68	.05
	Error	94.08	116	0.81		
2	Height Group	93.72	2	46.86	92.82	.05
	Error	59.07	117	0.50		
3	Height Group	3.92	2	1.96	2.18	n.s.
	Error	105.25	117	0.90		
4	Height Group	2.55	2	1.27	21.14	.05
	Error	6.97	116	0.06		
5	Height Group	7.07	2	3.53	3.10	n.s.
	Error	132.08	116	1.13		
6	Height Group	8.57	2	4.25	2.87	n.s.
	Error	173.81	117	1.48		
7	Height Group	15.21	2	7.60	7.38	.05
	Error	120.58	117	1.03		
8	Height Group	18.58	2	9.29	8.03	.05
	Error	135.58	117	1.15		
9	Height Group	31.12	2	15.56	15.63	.05
	Error	115.43	116	1.00		
10	Height Group	24.17	2	12.08	12.43	.05
	Error	113.70	117	0.97		
11	Height Group	3.66	2	1.83	2.41	n.s.
	Error	89.00	117	0.76		
12	Height Group	12.86	2	6.43	6.62	.05
	Error	113.64	117	1.17		
13	Height Group	3.13	2	1.56	1.33	n.s.
	Error	137.46	117	1.17		
14	Height Group	1.17	2	.59	0.49	n.s.
	Error	139.49	117	1.17		
15	Height Group	5.68	2	2.84	5.02	.05
	Error	66.18	117	0.56		
16	Height Group	2.78	2	1.39	1.87	n.s.
	Error	87.20	117	0.75		
17	Height Group	2.84	2	1.42	1.79	n.s.
	Error	92.33	116	0.80		

Notes: SS = sum of squares   F = F ratio
       df = degree of freedom   p = probability level
       MS = mean square   n.s. = not significant

In question 1 significant ANOVA results were attained [$F = 16.68(2,116)$, $p < .05$]. Tukey follow-up test results revealed a significant difference between the tall and short groups and the tall and average groups. No significant difference was found between the short and average groups. It is clear that taller subjects believe that their height has been a distinct asset in their social inter-

Table 5–3
Tukey Follow-Up Tests for Questionnaire Data

Question	Height Group			Comparisons
	Short	Average	Tall	
1	2.21	2.38	3.22[a]	T > S
		.26	1.10[a]	T > A
			.84[a]	S & A n.s.
2	1.28	1.53	3.24	S > T
		.25	1.96[b]	S > A
			1.71[b]	A & T n.s.
4	5.87	6.01	6.22	All Pairwise
		.1412[c]	.3530[c]	diff. sig.
			.21184[c]	T > A > S
7	2.31	3.00	3.10	A > S
		.69[d]	.79[d]	T > S
			.10	T & A n.s.
8	3.12	3.39	4.05	T > A
		.69	.79[e]	T > S
			.10	A & S n.s.
9	2.59	3.18	3.82	T > A > S
		.59[f]	1.23[f]	
			.64[f]	
10	2.57	3.21	3.65	A > S
		.64[g]	1.08[g]	T > S
			.44	T & A n.s.
12	2.45	2.58	3.19	S > T
		.13	.74[h]	S > A
			.61[h]	T & A n.s.
15	2.45	2.50	2.93	S > T
		.05	.48[i]	S > A
			.43[i]	T & A n.s.

Notes: T = tall
      S = short
      A = average
      n.s. = not significant
[a] $p < .05$, c.v. = .48
[b] $p < .05$, c.v. = .38
[c] $p < .05$, c.v. = .131
[d] $p < .05$, c.v. = .54
[e] $p < .05$, c.v. = .57
[f] $p < .05$, c.v. = .53
[g] $p < .05$, c.v. = .52
[h] $p < .05$, c.v. = .52
[i] $p < .05$, c.v. = .40

actions. Although the average and short subjects did not significantly differ from one another on this question, the short subjects did tend to have lower scores.

Significant ANOVA results were attained for question 2 [$F = 92.98(2,117)$, $p < .05$]. The Tukey follow-up test results indicated a significant difference between the short and tall groups and the short and average groups. The average and tall groups did not significantly differ from one another. The responses to question 2 reveal that both the tall and average subjects do not believe that their height has hindered them socially. The responses of these two groups fall between the never to rarely response categories. This is in direct contrast to their shorter counterparts who believe that their height has been a definite hindrance to them socially. The response of the short group falls between the sometimes to often categories. The trend is linear with the tallest subjects reporting the lowest frequency of hindrance, the average height subjects reporting a higher frequency, and the short subjects reporting the highest frequency.

Question 3: Do you ever add inches when reporting your height?

On this question, none of the three groups admitted to adding inches when reporting their height [$F = 2.18(2,117)$, n.s.]. The means for the three groups were clustered between the never and rarely response categories.

Question 4: If you could choose any height to be what would it be?

This question was included for the purpose of assessing the overall satisfaction that members of each group experience regarding their own height. The ANOVA results were significant [$F = 21.24(2,116)$, $p < .05$]. The Tukey (HSD) follow-up test revealed significant differences between all groups with the short subjects desiring the greatest height increase (M = 6.1 inches), the average subjects desiring a moderate height increase (M = 2.9 inches), and the tall subjects desiring the least increase in height (M = 1.1 inches).

The three groups did not all choose the cultural ideal for height (around 6'2") but, rather, the respective group means reflected that the short subjects wanted to be 5'9"; the average subjects, 6'0"; and the tall subjects, 6'2". The results reveal that the shortest group desired the greatest increase in height and the tallest group desired the least. These results are presented in figure 5–3.

Questions 5 through 11: The list below contains a number of social situations in which height comparisons might be made. Using the scale below, indicate to what extent you feel comfortable in each situation.

Of the seven hypothetical situations presented in the questionnaire, there were significant ANOVA results for four of them: question 7 [$F = 7.38(2,117)$, $p < .05$], question 8 [$F = 8.03(2,117)$, $p < .05$], question 9 [$F = 15.63(2,116)$,

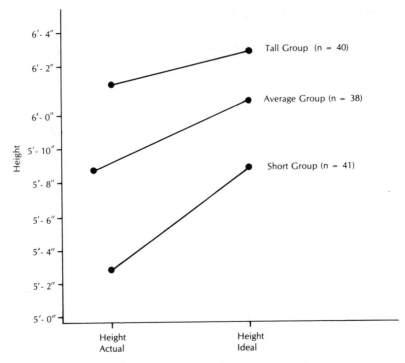

Figure 5–3. The Actual and Ideal Height for Short, Average, and Tall Males

$p < .05$], and question 10 [$F = 12.43(2,117)$, $p < .05$]. The Tukey follow-up test for question 7 indicates that subjects in the short group are significantly ($p < .05$) less comfortable on a first date than those in both the average and tall groups, while subjects in the tall and average groups did not significantly differ from one another. On question 8, the tall subjects reported being significantly more comfortable when involved in a contact sport than did either the average or short subjects. The responses to this question showed no significant difference between the average and short groups. This result probably reflects the importance of being taller than average for most competitive sports. The potential trend is as anticipated, with short subjects being least comfortable, average subjects being less comfortable, and tall subjects being most comfortable.

The Tukey follow-up test results for question 9 revealed that the tall subjects felt significantly ($p < .05$) more comfortable at a crowded party than did those in either the average or short groups. There was no significant difference between the average and short subjects on this item. The responses to question 10 revealed that both tall and average subjects were significantly more comfortable than were the short subjects when standing at a club or bar. It should be mentioned that for two of the three hypothetical situations in which no significant differences were found (questions 5 and 11), the means reveal that short subjects reported the least comfort, and tall subjects reported the most comfort. Overall, the subjects' responses to questions 5 through 11 reveal a significant difference in comfort level in social situations as a function of height, with the short subjects reporting the most discomfort.

Question 12: How important do you think a man's height is in acquiring a dating partner?

The results of the ANOVA for this question were significant [$F = 6.62(2,117)$, $p < .05$] with the Tukey follow-up test revealing that the short subjects significantly differed ($p < .05$) from both their tall and average counterparts. While short subjects felt that height was moderately important to very important in acquiring a dating partner, the tall and average subjects thought it only slightly to moderately important.

Question 13: How important do you think a man's height is in acquiring a marriage partner?

Unlike the findings for question 12 regarding dating partners, the respondents did not significantly differ in their reactions to this question [$F = 1.33(2,117)$, n.s.]. The entire group believes, on the average ($M = 2.14$), that height is not a terribly important factor in mate selection. It should be noted that the vast majority of subjects in this sample are unmarried (ninety-four percent). Also, given their relative youth, most undoubtedly have had little direct personal experience even seriously contemplating getting married.

Question 14: How important do you think a man's height is in being professionally successful in life?

The three height groups did not significantly differ in their opinions on this question [$F = 0.49(2,117)$, n.s.]. The mean score for all three groups clustered between the slightly important and moderately important categories (short: $M = 2.24$, SD = 1.00; average: $M = 2.47$, SD = 1.22; tall: $M = 2.30$, SD = 1.04). These results suggest that, in general, young men, regardless of their relative stature, perceive that height could be a factor in job success.

Question 15: Comparing your physical attractiveness with that of others of your sex and age, how attractive do you think you are?

The result of the ANOVA for question 15 was significant [$F = 5.02(2,117)$, $p < .05$], and the Tukey analyses revealed that the short subjects felt significantly ($p < .05$) less attractive than either the average or tall subjects. The average and tall subjects did not significantly differ from one another on this question.

Questions 16 and 17: Comparing your overall desirability as a dating partner (16) or marriage partner (17) with others of your sex and age, how desirable do you think you are?

There were no significant differences between the groups on questions 16 and 17 [$F(2,117) = 1.78$, n.s.: $F(2,117) = 1.79$, n.s.]. The whole group reported feeling somewhat more than average to average in desirability as dating and marriage partners (grand $M = 2.50$ for question 16, 2.35 for question 17).

In summary, the questionnaire results reveal that in many instances relative height plays a significant role in the way males feel about themselves. It is clear from the results that the subjects in this study believe that being taller is a social asset and, conversely, that short stature is a social liability. Moreover, the short subjects are more poignantly aware of the impact of height as they are the ones who must confront their difference within the social sphere on a daily basis. The responses to the seven hypothetical social situations (questions 5 through 11) highlighted this. In four of the seven situations, significant differences among the groups were attained, and the trend of tall subjects reporting greatest comfort and the short subjects reporting the least comfort was consistent, revealing the important role of height comparison within a social context.

The short males must negotiate a problem and, as anticipated, they are the ones who report the greatest awareness of potential issues. Apparently, short stature in males has some impact on their overall sense of attractiveness and desirability to females. It is also relevant to emphasize that while the short males in this study reported a desire for the most significant increase in height, even some of the tall subjects expressed a desire for a significant increase that would bring them to the height of the cultural ideal for males: 6′2″. All in all, the analysis of the questionnaire data indicates that most males, regardless of their height, report wanting to be significantly taller, and this confirms a cultural emphasis on stature and its probable relationship to other important life experience factors. If height were not such an important societal marker, the desire to exchange one height for another would not be so readily apparent.

Body Cathexis Scale Data

As can be seen in tables 5–4 and 5–5, the results of the ANOVA among the three height groups on the Body Cathexis Scale attained significance [$F =$

Table 5–4
Means and Standard Deviations for the Body Cathexis Scale

Group	Number	Mean	Standard Deviation
Short	41	2.73	.36
Average	40	2.48	.41
Tall	36	2.49	.57
All Subjects	117	2.57	.46

Table 5–5
ANOVA for Body Cathexis Scale

Source	SS	df	MS	F	p
Between Groups	1.64	2	.82	4.06	p < .01
Within Group	22.97	114	.20		

Notes: SS = sum of squares F = F ratio
   df   = degree of freedom p = probability level
   MS = mean square

4.06(2,114), p < .01]. The Tukey follow-up test results revealed that the short subjects differed significantly (p < .05) from the average and tall subjects (see table 5–6). In other words, the short subjects felt significantly less positive about their bodies than did the average and tall subjects. The average and tall groups were not significantly different from each other regarding their feelings about their bodies.

It is important to note that, although a significant difference was found, none of the groups report feeling negatively about their bodies. Rather, it is more accurate to say that the short males feel less positively about their bodies than do their taller peers.

Table 5–6
Tukey Multiple Range Test for Body Cathexis Scale

Mean	Group	Average	Short	Tall
2.48	Average			
2.73	Tall	a		a
2.49	Short	Short > Average Short > Tall		

^{a}p < .05

Semantic Differential Data

A 3 × 3 multiple analysis of variance (MANOVA) design was utilized for the semantic differential data. This design, as may be seen in table 5-7, has short subjects, average subjects, and tall subjects rating the three concepts: men of average height, men of short height, and men of tall height, across seventeen paired adjectives. In a MANOVA analysis, the F ratio is actually an approximation and cannot be directly ascertained (Tabachnick and Fidell 1983). Therefore, in this study, the Wilk's Lamda, from which the subsequent F ratio was derived, has also been reported. The F approximations given here were produced by the BMDP2V computer program (*SPSXX User's Guide* 1983).

Analysis of the main effects data among the groups indicates that the three height groups do not show a significant overall difference in their ratings of the semantic differential concepts [*Lamda* = .6497, F = 1.39(34,196), n.s.], that is, when the three rating scales are collapsed, the groups doing the rating do not significantly differ in their overall scores (see table 5-8).

Analysis of the main effects within each group for rated height reveals that there is significant agreement among the three subject groups regarding the three

Table 5-7
Semantic Differential 3 × 3 MANOVA Design

Height Groups	Men of Average Height	Men of Short Height	Men of Tall Height
Short Subjects	Q1-17	Q1-17	Q1-17
Average	Q1-17	Q1-17	Q1-17
Tall	Q1-17	Q1-17	Q1-17

Table 5-8
MANOVA Results for Semantic Differential Data

Source	Wilks Lamda	Approximate F	df	p
Between Groups Height	.65	1.39	34/196	n.s.
Within Groups Height	.28	11.05	34/424	< .001
Height × Height	.31	1.90	68/162	< .001

Notes: n.s. = not significant
F = F ratio
df = degree of freedom
p = probability level

concepts rated. That is, men of tall height, men of average height, and men of short height were rated differently [*Lamda* = .2812, F = 11.05(24,424), $p <$ .001]. The magnitude of this difference is graphically displayed in figure 5–4. Follow-up ANOVA's on the 17 items revealed significant effects for all but one of the items (item 3). Table 5–9 lists means and standard deviations for these data. The ANOVA results may be found in table 5–10.

The patterns seen in figure 5–4 may be summarized as follows: Men of tall and average height, as compared to men of short height, are seen as being significantly more mature, uninhibited, positive, secure, masculine, active, complete, successful, optimistic, dominant, capable, confident, and outgoing. The overall scores for the entire male sample strongly indicate that there is an at-

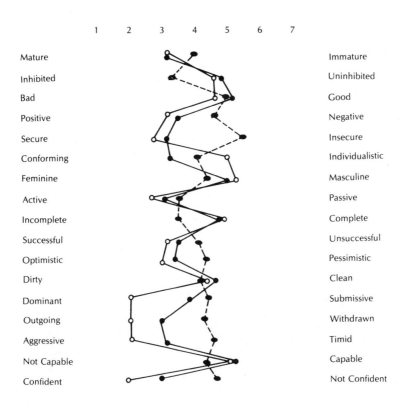

Key: ● Men of Average Height
 ◖ Men of Short Height
 ○ Men of Tall Height

Figure 5–4. Semantic Differential: Within Group Main Effects Ratings of Men of Short, Average, and Tall Height

Table 5–9
Semantic Differential: Within Group Main Effects

Paired Adjective	Average Height		Short Height		Tall Height	
	Mean	Standard Deviation	Mean	Standard Deviation	Mean	Standard Deviation
1	3.10	1.03	3.74	1.48	3.27	1.37
2	4.34	1.17	3.51	1.37	4.83	1.45
3	4.63	1.06	4.53	1.10	4.36	1.21
4	3.35	1.23	4.30	1.29	3.07	1.26
5	3.22	1.19	5.12	1.13	2.90	1.33
6	3.76	1.50	4.10	1.48	4.49	1.43
7	5.20	1.16	4.59	1.30	5.35	1.24
8	3.24	1.23	3.72	1.39	2.78	1.31
9	4.90	1.03	3.89	1.20	4.96	1.12
10	3.68	1.15	3.94	1.15	3.06	1.25
11	3.30	1.06	4.25	1.31	3.01	1.15
12	4.95	1.09	4.49	1.25	4.66	1.20
13	3.76	1.05	4.70	1.28	2.55	1.16
14	2.93	1.02	4.08	1.45	2.85	1.26
15	3.18	.98	4.16	1.53	2.73	1.19
16	5.09	1.05	4.50	1.31	4.95	1.08
17	3.10	1.18	4.48	1.37	2.63	1.22

tribution of more positively valenced personality traits and personal qualities to men of tall and average height. Conversely, men of short height are seen as possessing significantly fewer of these qualities.

Interaction Effects

Analysis of the Semantic Differential data reveals significant interaction effects, that is, the height of the subjects doing the ratings has some effect on the rating of the three concepts: men of average height, men of short height, and men of tall height [$F = 1.78(68,834)$, $p < .001$].

The scores on the seventeen-item Semantic Differential measures were collapsed in order to yield one composite score. As would be expected, the results, as seen in table 5–11 were the same as for the MANOVA. The main effect for subject group did not attain significance [$F = 0.50(2,114)$, n.s.], while the main effect for rated height did attain significance [$F = 105.99(2,114)$, $p < .001$].

The interaction of the two main effects was also significant [$F = 6.66(4,228)$, $p < .001$], and simple effects tests for this significant interaction were conducted

Table 5–10
Semantic Differential: ANOVA for Individual Items

Item	Source	SS	df	MS	F	p
1	Rated Height	26.18	2	13.09	8.55	<.001
	Error	361.41	236	1.53		
2	Rated Height	93.13	2	46.56	22.47	<.01
	Error	415.18	236	1.76		
3	Rated Height	4.26	2	2.13	2.28	n.s.
	Error	220.04	236	0.93		
4	Rated Height	101.14	2	50.56	34.79	<.01
	Error	345.93	238	1.45		
5	Rated Height	351.75	2	175.87	117.24	<.01
	Error	354.03	236	1.50		
6	Rated Height	31.94	2	15.97	7.49	<.001
	Error	507.50	238	2.13		
7	Rated Height	39.99	2	19.99	21.78	<.01
	Error	218.56	238	0.92		
8	Rated Height	53.31	2	26.65	16.83	<.01
	Error	373.77	236	1.58		
9	Rated Height	82.48	2	41.24	35.37	<.01
	Error	277.52	238	1.16		
10	Rated Height	46.17	2	23.08	19.72	<.01
	Error	278.66	238	1.17		
11	Rated Height	102.59	2	51.29	40.65	<.01
	Error	297.80	236	1.26		
12	Rated Height	14.73	2	7.36	7.10	<.001
	Error	247.11	238	1.03		
13	Rated Height	305.20	2	152.60	99.84	<.01
	Error	360.70	236	1.53		
14	Rated Height	113.25	2	56.62	37.29	<.01
	Error	383.00	236	1.51		
15	Rated Height	133.65	2	66.82	41.18	<.01
	Error	383.00	236	1.62		
16	Rated Height	22.47	2	11.33	12.26	<.001
	Error	218.17	238	0.92		
17	Rated Height	219.20	2	109.59	70.21	<.01
	Error	371.51	238	1.56		

Notes: SS = sum of squares F = F ratio
df = degrees of freedom p = probability level
MS = mean square n.s. = not significant

Table 5–11
Semantic Differential: ANOVA for Averaged Rating Scales

Source	SS	df	MS	F	p
Height Group	0.59	2	0.30	0.50	n.s.
Error	68.42	114	0.60		
Rated Height	68.77	2	34.39	105.99	<.001
Interaction	8.65	4	2.16	6.66	<.001
Error	73.98	228	0.32		

Notes: SS = sum of squares   F = F ratio
df = degrees of freedom   p = probability level
MS = mean square   n.s. = not significant

(Winer 1971). These results are contained in table 5–12. Regarding men of short height, a significant effect was found [$F = 3.52(2,312)$, $p < .05$] indicating that the subject groups significantly differed in their ratings. A Tukey follow-up test reveals that all those differences are significant ($p < .05$) except for the difference between short and average subjects.

Regarding the concept men of average height, no significant differences were found between groups [$F = 2.03(2,312)$, n.s.]. The means and standard deviations were as follows: short subjects (n = 40), (M = 3.39, SD = .869), average height subjects (n = 40), (M = 3.32, SD = .664), and tall subjects (n = 37), (M = 3.11, SD = .602). The overall results reveal that all three height groups attributed positively loaded adjective ratings to the concept of men of average height.

While all three groups responded with a relatively unfavorable attitude toward men of short height, the tall subjects report an especially negative attitude (see table 5–13). The means and standard deviations for the three subject groups ratings are as follows: short subjects (M = 3.89, SD = .467), average

Table 5–12
Simple Effect ANOVA for Semantic Differential Interaction Effects

Source	SS	df	MS	F	p
All Ss Rating Short	2.38	2	1.46	3.52	<.05
All Ss Rating Average	1.69	2	.85	2.03	n.s.
All Ss Rating Tall	4.63	2	2.31	5.55	<.01
Error	311.60	312	.42		

Notes: Ss = subjects   F = F ratio
SS = sum of squares   p = probability level
df = degree of freedom   n.s. = not significant
MS = mean square

Table 5–13
Men of Short Height: Semantic Differential Averaged Scales

	Subjects	
Short	Average	Tall
3.89	3.99	4.27
	.10	.38[a]
		.78[a]

[a]$p < .05$, c.v. = .20

height subjects (M = 3.99, SD = .601), and tall subjects (M = 4.27, SD = .735). These differences are graphically displayed in figure 5–5. The tall subjects view shorter males as being significantly more immature, conforming, incomplete, dirty, and not capable, than either of the other two subject groups.

There was also a significant difference in the way in which the groups rated men of tall height [F = 5.55(2,312), $p < .01$]. A Tukey follow-up test shows all pairwise differences are significant ($p < .05$) except for the difference between short and average subjects (see table 5–14). The mean scores and standard deviations are as follows: for short subjects (M = 3.08, SD = .736), average subjects (M = 3.40, SD = .601), and tall subjects (M = 2.73, SD = .739). The significant difference between the tall subjects' appraisal of men of tall height and that of the other two groups is rather striking and seems to be reflective of the generally more positive feeling that tall subjects have about their bodies as compared to shorter men. An analysis of the items reveals that the tall subjects view men of tall height as significantly more mature, uninhibited, good, positive, masculine, successful, optimistic, and capable than they do men of short height (see figure 5–6). Tall subjects are especially cathected to their own height category.

Table 5–14
Men of Tall Height: Semantic Differential Averaged Scales

	Subjects	
Short	Average	Tall
2.73	3.08	3.21
	.35	.48[a]
		.13[a]

[a]$p < .05$, c.v. = .20

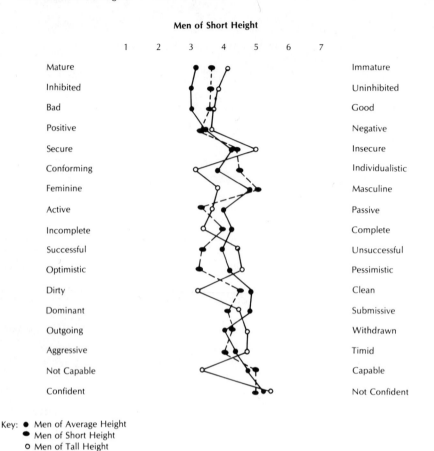

Men of Short Height

	1	2	3	4	5	6	7	
Mature								Immature
Inhibited								Uninhibited
Bad								Good
Positive								Negative
Secure								Insecure
Conforming								Individualistic
Feminine								Masculine
Active								Passive
Incomplete								Complete
Successful								Unsuccessful
Optimistic								Pessimistic
Dirty								Clean
Dominant								Submissive
Outgoing								Withdrawn
Aggressive								Timid
Not Capable								Capable
Confident								Not Confident

Key: ● Men of Average Height
⬮ Men of Short Height
○ Men of Tall Height

Figure 5–5. Semantic Differential: Men of Short Height

This result could be anticipated since being tall is such a highly valued physical characteristic.

Factor Scores

The Semantic Differential data were also collapsed along the Evaluation, Potency, and Activity factors as outlined by Osgood, Suci, and Tannenbaum (1957). The results of the ANOVA (see table 5–15) and Tukey follow-up tests for main effects reveal significant differences that are analogous to the results of the item-by-item and composite score analyses. The mean factor scores for rated height may be seen in table 5–16. The main effect for rated height on the Evaluation factor was significant [$F = 47.11(2,232)$, $p < .001$]. Tukey follow-up tests revealed that men of short height were seen less favorably on this factor than either

Men of Tall Height

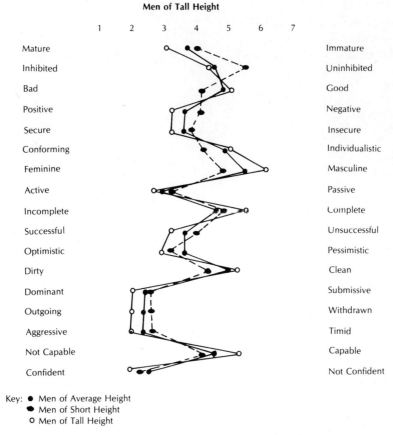

Key: ● Men of Average Height
    ◖ Men of Short Height
    ○ Men of Tall Height

Figure 5–6. Semantic Differential: Men of Tall Height

men of average height or men of tall height ($p < .05$). As previously discussed, the Evaluation factor refers to the construct of goodness.

The main effect for rated height on the Potency factor was also significant [$F = 88.25(2,236)$, $p < .001$]. The Tukey follow-up tests revealed that all pairwise differences are significant ($p < .05$) with men of tall height being seen as most potent, men of average height being seen as less potent than men of tall height, and men of short height being seen as the least potent. The Potency factor is interpreted as strength and is highly associated with perceived masculinity.

As with the main effects for the Evaluation and Potency factors, the main effect for rated height on the Activity factor was significant [$F = 37.11(2,234)$, $p < .001$]. All pairwise differences on the Activity factor are significant, with men of short height being seen as the least active or most passive, men of average height being seen as more active or less passive than men of short height, and

Table 5–15
ANOVAs for Semantic Differential Factor Scores

Source	SS	df	MS	F	p
Evaluation					
Rated Height	36.79	2	15.40	47.11	< .001
Error	90.60	232	0.39		
Potency					
Rated Height	135.98	2	67.99	88.25	< .001
Error	181.82	236	.77		
Activity					
Rated Height	71.96	2	35.98	37.11	< .001
Error	226.86	234	0.97		

Notes: SS = sum of squares   F = F ratio
       df = degree of freedom   p = probability level
       MS = mean square

Table 5–16
Semantic Differential: Mean Factor Scores for Main Effects

	Short Height		Average Height		Tall Height		
Factor	Mean	Standard Deviation	Mean	Standard Deviation	Mean	Standard Deviation	Tukey Follow-Up Test Summary
Evaluation	3.86	.54	3.19	.60	3.18	.63	S > T & A (p < .05)
Potency	4.13	.99	3.27	.64	2.64	1.05	All pairwise differences significant S > A > T (p < .05)
Activity	4.09	.78	3.46	.51	3.00	.62	All pairwise differences significant S > A > T (p < .05)

Notes: Number of subjects = 120.
       S = short
       T = tall
       A = average

men of tall height being seen as the most active or least passive (see tables 5–15 and 5–16).

In addition, with the exception of the Activity factor, significant interactions on the factor scores were also found [$F = 9.66(4,236)$, $p < .001$]. These results are presented in table 5–17. The simple effects test on the Potency factor reveals

Table 5–17
ANOVA of Interaction Effects for Semantic Differential Factor Scores

Source	SS	df	MS	F	p
Evaluation					
Interaction	15.10	4	3.77	9.66	p < .001
Error	90.60	232	0.39		
Potency					
Interaction	10.20	4	2.55	3.31	p < .05
Error	181.82	236	.77		
Activity					
Interaction	2.08	4	0.52	0.54	n.s.
Error	226.86	234	0.97		

Notes: SS = sum of squares   F = F ratio
df = degrees of freedom   p = probability level
MS = mean square   n.s. = not significant

that short subjects significantly differentiate between the height categories [$F = 15.87(2,236)$, $p < .001$]. The Tukey follow-up test reveals that men of short height are rated as less potent by short subjects than either of the other two height designations. This result is probably indicative of the relatively low body cathexis and body satisfaction found among short men.

The simple effects test concerning the Potency factor for average height subjects was significant [$F = 30.58(2,236)$, $p < .001$]. The results of the Tukey follow-up test reveal that the average height subjects rate the short subjects as least potent while not significantly differentiating between men of average height and men of tall height. The simple effects test on the Potency factor for tall subjects was significant [$F = 48.03(2,236)$, $p < .001$]. The Tukey follow-up test revealed that men of short height are viewed by the tall subjects as least potent. The tall subjects also rated men of average height as significantly less potent than men of tall height. The tall subjects felt particularly positive about men of tall height which most likely reflects their own generally high degree of body satisfaction and positive body cathexis.

The interaction between the subjects' heights and the rated height on the Evaluation factor was found to be significant [$F = 9.66(4,232)$, $p < .001$]. On the Evaluation factor the short subjects did not differ in how they rated the three height categories [$F = 2.71(2,232)$, n.s.], but the other two subject groups did respond differentially as a function of height designations. The average subjects differentiated between the three height categories on the Evaluation factor [$F = 14.79(2,232)$, $p < .001$], and the Tukey follow-up test reveals that they rated men of short height significantly lower than either of the other two groups. For the tall subjects, the results of the simple effects test were also significant [$F = 48.38(2,232)$, $p < .001$]. The Tukey follow-up test analyses reveal that tall

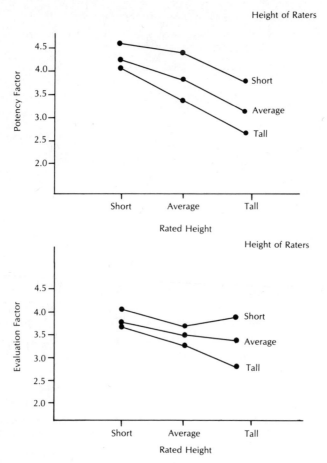

Figure 5–7. Semantic Differential: Simple Effects Tests for Factor Scores

subjects rated men of short height least positively, men of average height more positively, and men of tall height most positively. All pairwise differences are significant. The tall subjects had a particularly unfavorable opinion of short males (see figure 5–7).

Activity Vector Analysis (AVA) Data

One of the predictions posited in this study was that men of different heights will vary on the construct of self-concept as assessed by the Activity Vector Analysis (AVA). The individual subject profiles were scored according to the directions outlined in the *Manual for the Activity Vector Analysis* (1973) with the raw scores, converted scores, pattern shapes, activity scores, and congruence indexes calculated for each subject.

As noted earlier in this chapter, within the AVA system a pattern shape refers to one of 258 specific coded AVA profiles, and each profile reflects the relative strength and magnitude of each of four vectors: aggressiveness, sociability, emotional stability, and social adaptability. The profiles are coded on a scale of one through nine with the ipsative mean being set at five. There must be at least a one or a nine in the coded pattern. The sum of them must equal twenty. Under these constraints there can be only 258 pattern shapes.

Prior to the analysis of the AVA, the individual profiles were inspected for elevation and scatter. The scatter was determined by examining the deviation ratios and the graphs of pattern shapes. The deviation ratio is obtained by dividing the highest vector score by the lowest vector score on the self, role, and image profiles. A resulting deviation ratio of less than 1.0 does not allow a confident analysis of the comparative vector strength within the integration. Such subject profiles were not included in the analysis. As noted in the AVA manual it is at that point, with all vectors at about the ipsative mean, that the subject's behavior is difficult to describe. Conversely, a deviation ratio of 1.85 or larger indicates a degree of evasion. In addition, pattern shapes based on too few adjectives checked (less than six) or too many (more than seventy) were not included. In all, only five profiles were excluded from data analysis.

Six dimensions of self-concept, as measured by the AVA, were utilized in this study. The first dimension is the *social self* which is defined as an individual's perception of how he feels he is being seen by others. It is the self-concept through which a person perceives how he needs to behave in order to meet the demands of social living. The second dimension is the *basic self* which is defined as an individual's perception of how he really thinks he sees himself. The third dimension is the *image* which is how the person is likely to be perceived by others. Fourth is the *ideal self* or the subject's view of the perfect person. Fifth is *congruence* which is a measure of the consistency between an individual's social self and his basic self. Finally, there is the dimension of *activity* which refers to the degree of aliveness, vitality, energy, or responsiveness to the environment.

Individual responses were scored in accordance with the specific guidelines described in the AVA manual. Activity scores were obtained by simply counting the total number of responses checked and then transcribing this number to the converted score (standard score scale with M = 50 and SD = 10). Scoring for each vector is obtained by counting the number of responses that load on that particular vector and then transforming the raw score to the converted score. The congruence score, which is defined as the relationship between the variables of the pattern shapes for the social self and basic self, is obtained by calculating the Pearson-type correlation between the two profiles.

The social self (role), basic self, image and ideal self constructs are analyzed by comparing group centroids for each of the three height groups on these constructs. The first analysis completed was that of the basic self. For the average height group, the centroid was the pattern shape 4349. Thirty-three percent of the subjects were included within this cluster. The profile 4349 falls squarely within the influence of vector 4. Individuals within the influence of a high vector 4 may be described as cautious, suggestible, compliant, and conforming. They may be viewed as dependent-follower personalities. They are not generally leaders, and they perform best and feel most comfortable in situations which call for strict adherence to rules or instructions (*Manual for the AVA* 1973).

The short height group profiles for the basic self also clustered solidly within the vector 4 influence. In fact, forty-nine percent of the short group were included within this cluster, reflecting a tighter grouping than that of the average subjects, that is, a greater number of the short subjects were more distinctly within the influence of the high vector 4 pattern. In contrast, analysis of the tall subject profiles for the basic self revealed a wide dispersion with no identifiable clusters, reflecting much greater variance than either of the other two groups.

Analysis of the social self (role) data reveals that thirty-eight percent of the average subject profiles cluster about pattern shape 6815. This cluster yields a high vector 2 and low vector 3 influence. The individual who fits this profile may be described as sociable, gracious, and persuasive. He is enthusiastic, but he is also the kind of person who may get carried away by his own hearty manner and high spirits. Because of this, he may at times be considered a thoughtless person.

The short subject profiles on the social self clustered around pattern shape 4349. Forty percent of the short subjects were included within this cluster. This pattern shape is well within the influence of vector 4, and it is basically the same as the pattern for this group's basic self image. As already mentioned, the person who fits this profile is highly dependent on others for guidance, assurance, and direction. He finds it difficult to make independent decisions and works best when instructions and directions are laid down. He is anxious and is likely to be a worrier, especially about his own actions. These people have a strong tendency to be meticulous, fastidious, and punctilious. They do careful and accurate work, and they take great precautions not to deviate from established rules and guidelines. In contrast, the pattern shapes of tall subjects on the social self were once again scattered with no highly distinct clusters.

On the image construct, the average subjects were divided between two clusters. The pattern shape centroids for these two clusters were 4349 and 4817. It is important to note that these two centroids are not polar opposites but do share the common element of a low vector 3 influence. People who fit into these pattern shapes are very expressive. They tend not to worry about things until they happen, and do not plan well due to their impulsiveness.

The short subjects were once again clustered within the high vector 4 influence on the image construct. This group centroid of pattern shape 5429 included fifty-four percent of the short subjects, making it a rather tight cluster. This pattern shape reflects a high vector 4 and low vector 3 influence indicating that a majority of the short subjects have an image of themselves reflecting the need for dependency, guidance, assurance, and structure.

The tall subjects were without a distinct cluster on the image construct. As with the basic self and social self results for this group, the majority of pattern shapes (ninety-two percent) were quite scattered. It should be noted that in the normative sample of the AVA there is approximately equal saturation throughout the AVA universe. The sample of tall subjects, then, is rather different from the general population on this measure, but it was clear that a great many tall individuals were assertive and independent while not as people-oriented. Many were calm, reflective, and obviously leader types.

What is particularly interesting in the AVA results is the pronounced consistency in the basic self, social self, and image profiles for the short group. While the average group is similar to the short group on the basic self profile, they believe that they present a more sociable façade to others than is reflected in their basic self profile. They also believe that others see them that way. The short subjects, on the other hand, think of themselves as highly dependent, and they believe that others see them this way. In fact, the image profile for the short subjects, according to them, is the way they think others perceive them. Given the predominant influence of vector 4 on the basic, social, and image profiles, one would expect short individuals to be more contained, take fewer interpersonal risks, and be more concerned about how others see them than would be the case for taller individuals. Such an interpretation is generally consistent with the results from the other measures in this study.

The analysis of the ideal self data for the subjects in the present study is rather provocative in that it does not mirror the results of previous AVA research. Previous research with the AVA has found that the ideal male self-concept is that of a Jack Armstrong, All-American Boy stereotype (e.g., Merenda 1964, Merenda and Clarke 1959b, Merenda and Mohan 1966, Merenda and Shapurian 1974). This ideal type of person may be described as

> one who is at his best in a situation requiring smooth performance. He is relatively passive but friendly and is widely attracted to a wide variety of people. He is a charmer who is politically astute and is successful in getting others to go along with his view (Merenda and Shapurian 1974, p. 1208).

In the present study, the analysis of ideal self data reveal that there is a remarkable similarity among the short, average, and tall groups. The composite profile of the entire sample clustered about pattern shape 4871. This pattern is fairly similar to previous findings but also indicates more concern for the feelings of others than was reflected in the ideal self patterns of male college students in earlier studies (e.g., Merenda 1964, Merenda and Clarke 1967, Merenda and Shapurian 1974).

A person with AVA pattern shape 4871 (the modal pattern for ideal self in the present study) may be described as having a gregarious, sociable and empathic attitude toward the needs of others. He has a great deal of personal appeal, and he gives the impression of being genuinely interested in other people. He is a warm and friendly person who has the capability to make others feel comfortable in his presence. This pattern shape reflects a high vector 3 influence, and this finding was consistent across the three groups. This profile reflects what appears to be the integration of traits that have traditionally been thought of as "feminine" and "masculine," that is, we may be seeing a movement toward androgeny becoming a more valued ideal among male college students (Kaplan and Sedney 1980, Sargent 1977, Singer 1976).

Women's Perceptions

In order to find out whether women viewed men differently as a function of their stature, results of their responses to the Semantic Differential Measures were also analyzed. The subjects were 120 female college students who represented the entire female population of an introductory psychology course at a large New England university. They were classmates of one of the groups of males who participated in the research project described earlier in this chapter and responded to the same procedures, including the Semantic Differential Measures. Almost ninety-eight percent of the subjects were single, ninety-five percent were Caucasian, and they were primarily from middle-class backgrounds.

Item-by-item analyses of variance among the three Semantic Differentials were performed utilizing the BMDP2V computer program (*SPSXX User's Guide* 1983). The ANOVAs revealed highly significant differences ($p < .01$) across fifteen of the seventeen items. The ANOVA results appear in table 5–18. Significant ANOVAs were followed up by the Tukey multiple range test. These results are presented in table 5–19.

The pattern of results across items on the three measures is graphically illustrated in figure 5–8. As the pattern of individual items clearly indicates, the female subjects had remarkably distinct and unequivocal opinions about the characteristics associated with men of different heights. The men of short height were consistently seen in pejorative or negatively valenced terms while the men of average height and men of tall height were seen in consistently positive terms. As may be seen in table 5–19 the vast majority of responses yield no significant difference between men of tall height and men of average height. On the other

Table 5–18
Female Responses: ANOVAs for Individual Items
on Semantic Differential

Item	Source	SS	df	MS	F	p
1	Rated Height	118.96	2	59.48	31.99	<.01
	Error	673.04	362	1.86		
2	Rated Height	159.44	2	79.72	34.68	<.01
	Error	804.56	350	2.30		
3	Rated Height	4.63	2	2.32	2.07	n.s.
	Error	401.37	358	1.12		
4	Rated Height	351.92	2	175.96	115.80	<.01
	Error	550.07	362	1.52		
5	Rated Height	689.43	2	344.72	194.89	<.01
	Error	633.23	358	1.77		
6	Rated Height	95.22	2	47.61	18.27	<.05
	Error	938.12	360	2.60		
7	Rated Height	123.15	2	61.57	46.04	<.01
	Error	481.51	360	1.33		
8	Rated Height	122.58	2	61.19	35.03	<.01
	Error	632.22	362	1.74		
9	Rated Height	140.66	2	95.33	68.38	<.01
	Error	504.67	362	1.39		
10	Rated Height	90.89	2	45.44	30.94	<.01
	Error	531.77	362	1.46		
11	Rated Height	257.45	2	128.73	83.43	<.01
	Error	558.55	362	1.54		
12	Rated Height	1.60	2	.80	.89	n.s.
	Error	321.06	358	.90		
13	Rated Height	473.30	2	236.65	120.65	<.01
	Error	710.03	362	1.96		
14	Rated Height	284.65	2	142.33	87.34	<.01
	Error	586.67	360	1.63		
15	Rated Height	314.42	2	157.21	91.55	<.01
	Error	614.91	362	1.69		
16	Rated Height	73.55	2	36.77	26.42	<.01
	Error	501.11	360	1.39		
17	Rated Height	581.09	2	291.04	155.57	< .01
	Error	677.24	362	1.87		

Notes: SS = sum of squares   F = F ratio
        df = degrees of freedom   p = probability level
        MS = mean square   n.s. = not significant

Table 5–19
Female Responses: Tukey Follow-Up Tests for Semantic Differential Items

Item Number	Rated Height (RH)			Comparisons
	Tall	Average	Short	
1	3.07	3.12 .05	4.08 1.01[a] .96	Short > Tall and Average
2	3.38	4.48 1.10	4.59 1.21[b] .11	Short < Tall and Average
4	2.58	2.83 .25	4.40 1.82[c] 1.57	Short > Tall and Average
5	2.67	2.85 .18	5.15 2.48[d] 2.30	Short > Tall and Average
6	4.01	4.07 .06	4.92 .91[e] .85	Tall > Short and Average
7	4.4	5.35 .91[f]	5.52 1.08[f] .17	Short < Average and Tall
8	2.73	2.87 .14	3.80 1.07[g] .93	Short > Tall and Average
9	3.98	5.07 1.09[h]	5.35 1.37[h] .28	Short < Average and Tall
10	2.90	2.92 .02	3.77 .87[i] .85	Short > Tall and Average
11	2.82	2.96 .15	4.34 1.53[j] 1.38[j]	Short > Tall and Average
13	2.45	3.26 .81[k]	4.70 2.25[k] 1.44	Tall < Average < Short
14	2.58	2.58	4.12 1.54[l] 1.54	Short > Average and Tall

Table 5-19 continued

Item Number	Rated Height (RH)			Comparisons
	Tall	Average	Short	
15	2.59	2.96	4.35	Tall > Average > Short
		.37^m	1.76^m	
			1.39	
16	4.70	5.34	5.56	Tall and Average > Short
		.64^n	.86^n	
			.22	
17	2.42	2.81	4.78	Tall > Average > Short
		.39°	2.36^o	
			1.97	

$^a p < .05$, c.v. = .340 $^i p < .05$, c.v. = .302
$^b p < .05$, c.v. = .384 $^j p < .05$, c.v. = .310
$^c p < .05$, c.v. = .307 $^k p < .05$, c.v. = .349
$^d p < .05$, c.v. = .333 $^l p < .05$, c.v. = .319
$^e p < .05$, c.v. = .403 $^m p < .05$, c.v. = .325
$^f p < .05$, c.v. = .289 $^n p < .05$, c.v. = .295
$^g p < .05$, c.v. = .329 $^o p < .05$, c.v. = .341
$^h p < .05$, c.v. = .294

hand, men of short height were viewed as much more inadequate than their taller counterparts.

Female subjects found men of short height to be more immature, inhibited, negative, insecure, conforming, feminine, passive, incomplete; and less successful, pessimistic, withdrawn, and capable than either men of average height or men of tall height. On three of the items, there were significant differences among all three height categories, with men of tall height seen as most dominant, aggressive, and confident; men of average height significantly less so; and men of short height the least so. On none of the seventeen items were men of short height rated more favorably than either of the other two categories (see figure 5-8).

The data were also collapsed along the Evaluation, Potency, and Activity factors. The results of the ANOVA and Tukey follow-up tests for the three factor scores reveal significant differences that are analogous to the results of the item-by-item ANOVA. The results for the Evaluation factor, as seen in table 5-20, reveal that the men of short height are evaluated in a significantly less favorable light than are either of the other two groups ($p < .01$).

In terms of the Potency factor, all pairwise differences are significant ($p < .05$) with men of tall height seen as most potent, men of average height seen as

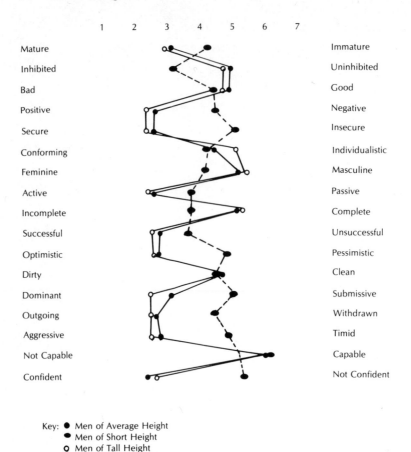

Figure 5–8. **Female Response Pattern for Individual Items on Semantic Differentials**

significantly less potent, and men of short height seen as least potent. Regarding the Activity factor, men of short height are viewed as significantly less active or more passive than their taller counterparts. All in all, the results of analyses of the factor scores parallel the item-by-item results, yielding uniformly consistent results.

These results clearly indicate that college-age, Caucasian females possess strong and consistently negative attitudes about men of short height. While previous research on height and its relationship to dating and marital choice has suggested that stereotyping and social discrimination does exist, rarely has this finding been seen as dramatically as in this study. Women's perceptions can have a very significant impact on the psychosocial development of short men.

Table 5–20
Female Responses: ANOVAs for Semantic Differential Factor Scores

Source	SS	df	MS	F	p
Evaluation					
Rated Height	97.70	2	48.85	96.33	<.001
Error	178.49	352	.51		
Potency					
Rated Height	280.19	2	140.09	140.26	<.001
Error	359.58	360	0.99		
Activity					
Rated Height	137.85	2	68.93	59.01	<.001
Error	408.80	350	1.17		

Notes: SS = sum of squares   F = F ratio
df = degrees of freedom   p = probability level
MS = mean square

Pattern of Adjustment

Although the patterning of their psychological and social functioning was clearly influenced by negative feedback and experiences concerning their relative stature, the short men in our research should not be viewed as emotionally disturbed or as suffering from serious psychopathology. It is relevant to reemphasize that all our subjects were attending college and, for the most part, were academically successful and generally seemed to be adequately coping with the demands of undergraduate living.

Individuals who reported medical difficulties or physical abnormalities were not included in the data analyses. In addition, the mean scores of all three of the height groups on Maslow's (1952) brief paper and the pencil measure of general psychological adjustment were well within the "normal range," with the short men's scores not being significantly different from those of the average or tall subjects (Martel 1985, Martel and Biller 1986).

The short men in our study were from middle-class backgrounds, and more than half were attending an Ivy League school. In terms of the educational expectations for people of their age, many were exceptionally successful. If we had chosen to study short males in the seventeen- to twenty-two-year-old range who were from middle-class (or lower-class) backgrounds but not able to attend college, it is highly likely that, as a group, their overall level of adjustment would have been much less adequate than was the case for our sample of short males.

Many factors influence both the patterning and quality of adjustment of short males and may either increase or decrease the probability of their manifesting psychopathology. A major goal of the next chapter is to further elaborate on a holistic-transactional framework for understanding the impact of stature and stigma on psychosocial development.

6
Overview and Clinical Implications

This chapter presents an integration of the data described in chapter 5 with the results of earlier research discussed in chapters 1 through 4. It also includes findings from our in-depth interviews with short men (Martel and Biller 1986). This chapter focuses on constructing a developmental and clinical framework for understanding specific issues in the psychological functioning of short men. There is a holistic-transactional perspective emphasizing both biosocial and family systems factors.

Our definition of short men has focused on those in the 5'2" to 5'5" range. Certainly males who are 5'6" or even 5'7", 5'8" or taller may experience some of the same concerns regarding self-perceptions of inferior stature but usually to a lesser degree. Moreover, it is apparent that, although men of average height (5'8" to 5'11") may feel at somewhat of a disadvantage in certain areas relative to taller men, their experience is generally quite different from that of short males.

Self-Acceptance

The results of our study supported the prediction that short males would be significantly less satisfied with the overall appearance of their bodies than either of the two other height groups. The degree of body satisfaction did not significantly differ between the average and tall groups but short college men did, in fact, experience less satisfaction with their bodies than did their taller peers. Moreover, the finding that the tall and average subjects do not significantly differ in their overall body cathexis scores supports the idea that height, as a predictor of body satisfaction, diminishes in importance when a man is of at least average stature. Those who are significantly below the cultural ideal for height are most aware of the role that insufficient stature plays, thereby affecting the view that they hold of themselves.

The short male's vulnerability to feelings of bodily inadequacy seems to be a function of his height relative to females as well as to other males. Much of the male's self-concept development is often, unfortunately, based on trying to be as different from females as possible (Biller 1971, 1974). It is important to note that men who are less than 5'6" are especially likely to encounter social situations in which they are shorter than most, if not all, of the women. On the other hand, males who are 5'6" to 5'8", though shorter than average for their sex, are likely to be taller than more than half of the females they meet.

The prediction that short males would demonstrate a less favorable self-concept was also substantially supported. What is most striking about the Activity Vector Analysis results is the way in which the short subject group's pattern shapes for basic self, social self, and image all clustered within the vector 4 influence. Such was not the case for the other two height groups. That is, the short group's centroids for these three assessments were virtually the same, indicating that they viewed themselves, felt others viewed them, and were likely to be viewed by others as dependent-follower personalities. This can be interpreted to mean that short subjects have a pronounced tendency to be more interpersonally constrained and are apt to take fewer interpersonal risks. They are likely to be the kind of individuals who are very concerned about how others see them. As a result, short males are less apt to take on leader roles. The leader role would require both interpersonal risk and assertive behavior which most of the short men in our study perceived to be incompatible with their self-image.

This result fits well with much of the previous literature (see chapters 1 through 4). The short male grows up perceiving his body, and having others perceive his body, as less than satisfactory. During pivotal developmental years when acceptance of the body as a symbol of the self is especially crucial, the short male may feel less secure about taking interpersonal risks, he is typically less competent in competitive sports, and he is not as successful in gaining peer acceptance, as compared to his taller peers. All in all, the short male is unlikely to feel that his body is a positive symbol of the self. It should not be unexpected, therefore, that the short male perceives himself as having a dependent-follower personality. Compared to the taller subjects, the short subjects viewed themselves as more withdrawn and self-conscious and believed that others see them this way. It should be pointed out, however, that the subjects in the study did not show any indications of pronounced psychopathology. Rather height was a factor in the style of psychological adjustment they developed. For the short subjects, their relative stature generally limited their range of adaptation; they appeared constricted and defensive in their adaptation rather than emotionally disturbed.

The average subjects demonstrated greater variability among the basic self, social self, and image constructs than did the short subjects. As with the short subjects, many of them saw themselves as having a dependent-follower personality, but in most cases they believed that others saw them as more sociable and outgoing. The results of the image profile were consistent with this belief. This is an important difference from the short group because it suggests greater flexibility and social skills. The tall subjects were the most variable group with respect to their Activity Vector Analysis pattern, having no clearly identifiable clusters. The tall subjects also felt most positively about themselves on the Body Cathexis Scale and the Semantic Differential Measure. Taking these results together, the implication is that the tall subjects represent a wide range of generally positive personality adaptations. Being tall, in a sense, may provide individuals with relative freedom in developing their unique characteristics, whereas short males may be burdened with working out feelings connected to their inadequate stature.

Regarding the ideal self-concept, the three height groups did agree on what characteristics the ideal person would possess. It appears that what are thought of as ideal male traits are undergoing a rather major shift. Unlike previous AVA self-concept studies, the present subjects no longer aspired to attain the Jack Armstrong, All-American Boy ideal. Rather, the ideal self-concept that this group chose was an individual who is not just superficially sociable, but has a genuine interest in other people, that is, the broader social changes in male and female roles seem to be influencing the male view of what is masculine. John Naisbett (1984), author of *Megatrends* and a researcher who follows such changes in American life, commented that just such a change was indeed a trend. Naisbett believes that a greater proportion of young men are adopting more traditionally feminine characteristics such as interpersonal sensitivity. He asserts that this readjustment of sex roles is "probably the most important thing that's going on in this century in America" (p. 104). This may be reflected by our results concerning ideal self-concepts.

Day-to-Day Issues

The prediction was supported that self-reported thoughts about the impact of height on an individual's daily life would be significantly more pronounced for the short male. The short subjects responded that their height had significantly hindered them. In contrast, the tall and average subjects did not experience height as limiting them socially.

In the seven hypothetical situations aimed at assessing self-perceived comfort in circumstances where height comparisons might be made, four significant results were attained. Tall subjects reported the greatest comfort and short subjects reported the least comfort, revealing the important role of height comparison within the social context. In none of the seven hypothetical situations did short subjects report greater comfort than the other two groups.

These results supported the prediction that short subjects would experience less comfort or security in social situations and are consistent with the previous literature on self-esteem, power, and issues relating to height within the social context. Within the social context the short male must directly confront his own feelings about being shorter than others and must negotiate the derisive comments and behavior of others. The short subjects' greater awareness of the importance of height in everyday life was rather dramatically reflected in their desire for the greatest amount of increase in height (mean = 6.1 inches).

As anticipated, short subjects believed significantly more strongly than the taller subjects that a man's height was important in acquiring a dating partner. The other two height groups did not feel it was as important, once again indicating their lack of emphasis on their own height as a key issue in their heterosexual encounters.

The impact of stature on the individual's belief regarding his attractiveness vis-à-vis his peers revealed that short subjects felt significantly less attractive. This result is consistent with differences on the Body Cathexis Scale, indicating the relatively low body satisfaction of short males. It is likely that this self-perception of being less attractive is due, in large part, to the consistently negative feedback that the short male receives from others regarding his physical appearance. As he matures, the short male begins to view himself more and more as others see him.

Perhaps most important for the self-concept development of short males is the way females view them. The results clearly indicated that the female subjects had strong and consistently negative attitudes regarding men of short height. On the other hand, men of average height and men of tall height were seen in consistently positive terms. The female subjects found men of short height to be more immature, inhibited, negative, insecure, conforming, feminine, passive, incomplete, pessimistic, withdrawn; and less successful and capable than either their average or taller male counterparts. On three of the items there were significant differences among all three height categories, with men of tall height seen as most dominant, aggressive, and confident; men of average height less so; and men of short height the least so. On none of the seventeen items were men of short height rated more favorably that either of the other two categories. When data was collapsed along the Evaluation, Potency, and Activity factors, men of short height were rated more negatively in every case.

Similar to their male counterparts, females tend to believe that men of short stature are not as attractive or masculine as their taller peers. Unfortunately, what Beigel (1954) wrote thirty years ago may be as true now as it was then: "Shorter males, as a rule, do not strike the female as true men" (p. 268). Our results clearly suggest that stereotyping, social discrimination, and attribution of personality characteristics based exclusively on height do, in fact, exist.

Interview Study

Twenty short college males (between 5'2" and 5'5") were interviewed regarding the possible developmental problems and everyday issues confronting them

(Martel and Biller, 1986). It is important to emphasize that these short males were relatively well-functioning in many areas, including being successful upper middle class students at a prestigious ivy league college. As a group, however, the short subjects presented a very strong awareness that their height made them significantly different than their taller counterparts. All reported an awareness that their short stature had a profound impact on their development, personality, and self-concept. All were aware that they had to compensate, in some way, for their stature.

The following excerpt from one interview serves to illustrate this point:

Interviewer: What kind of judgements do you think other people make about you based more or less exclusively on your height?

Subject: They are probably looking to see what I'm going to do to compensate for what I think my faults are in being short.

Interviewer: Why would you think that one has to compensate for this?

Subject: Because . . . there is something lacking and physically it's height. . . . Something needs to be compensated for.

Interviewer: Do you compensate for it?

Subject: Maybe I do. I make a conscious effort not to stand very close to other people. I also make sure that I am standing perfectly straight.

Interviewer: Why do you think it is so important?

Subject: Because from the beginning, you want to present as standard a view of yourself as possible.

Interviewer: What do you mean, standard?

Subject: You want to be as middle-of-the-road in everything until you get to see what this person you're confronting likes and dislikes. If I'm meeting someone who is short and I get the impression that he's comfortable, then I'm automatically comfortable. If he's shorter than I am, I won't make every effort to stand perfectly straight. If I'm meeting someone who is very tall and who is comfortable, then I'll be comfortable. If he's slouching, I'll probably still stand up straight.

This exchange was quite typical, revealing many of the elements of coping with short stature commented on in other chapters of this book. The subject is interpersonally wary, concerned about his difference, and expresses a greater defensiveness than the question seems to call for.

Below are some additional excerpts from the interview study which reveal the poignant flavor of feelings and reactions that often evolve in the short male.

Interviewer: Did you experience any problems because of it? I'm thinking of elementary school years.

Subject: Yeah, in terms of, there was always the typical picking of teams, and I was always one of kind of the smaller people who were just the last to be picked and, in general, people not realizing that you are as old as you are.

Interviewer: Why is it a problem if people would pick you last?

Subject: Just that for no other reasons than you were shorter. It was as though you were just inherently worse than everyone for no fault of your own, and people who were your friends regularly, in certain things like that, said, "Well, we don't want you."

Interviewer: Do you think that there is any relationship between the fact that you are shorter than average and brighter than average?

Subject: I don't know if there is any inherent relationship to start with. Maybe because, if you're shorter, and tend toward some sort of social isolation. You tend to study more in your early years.

Interviewer: Do you feel that you have been abused or mistreated in any way because of your height?

Subject: Oh, yeah, especially in elementary school. They said, "There's the fat kid, or the short kid."

Interviewer: Did you have a nickname?

Subject: Just the general "shortie." In terms of what bosses do, it seems that my perception of people is that, if they need to hire someone to be in charge of other people, they are more likely to hire someone who is the tall, domineering type person.

Interviewer: How would life be different for you if you were 5'10"?

Subject: In general, in relations with people, there would be one less obstacle, one less barrier you would have to overcome, or one less touchy subject to deal with in terms of meeting people.

Interviewer: Would you say that you come from a happy family, a well-adjusted family?

Subject: Oh, sure. My parents instilled a sense of self-esteem in what I was doing. It wasn't a sticky point that I wasn't playing basketball, because I was good at other things. I was particularly involved in leadership in my high school. Some people joked about that—Napoleon complex.

Interviewer: What do you think about people saying something like that?

Subject: Smaller people *have* to sort of fight their way through the crowd to be noticed. In some cases they have to be more defensive or more aggressive as the circumstances warrant. They tend to be the smarter people in the class, or people who are doers.

Interviewer: When was the first time that you became aware that you were not going to grow anymore?

Subject: When I was about twelve, they sent me to Boston Children's Hospital, ninth grade, to find out why. I went through all those painful tests for them to tell me that it was hereditary. It was very painful. I was angry that I had to go through all of those tests. But, I remember that I had feelings that my (younger) brother was bigger and stronger than I was. In terms of sibling rivalry, fights and things like that, he had power over me. I resented that.

Interviewer: First awareness. How did it feel?

Subject: Sixth grade. The first girl that I liked was 5'10". In gym, I was always the shortest. It didn't feel good. I remember feeling inferior. I remember thinking that if I got into any fights, 'cause I was in a rough school, I would lose, 'cause most everybody was bigger than me. So I would really never get involved in fights.

Interviewer: How did your not being as big as the other boys have an impact on your style or your relationships with them?

Subject: Oh, I was more verbal. I compensated verbally. I compensated in that way 'cause I was not really active in sports. They usually picked the bigger people on teams and that sort of thing, so I compensated verbally. I was very verbal and very hyper. So, in those ways, I think that's how I got my attention.

Interviewer: Do people call you cute frequently?

Subject: Yes. They still do, and it makes me angry.

Interviewer: In terms of competition . . .

Subject: I felt that I couldn't compete. I always felt—don't even try out for sports. There is no sense in even doing it.

Interviewer: How did you feel in gym class?

Subject: I always felt badly. I felt uncomfortable when they picked teams. I was always picked last.

Interviewer: Do you recall any feelings about that?

Subject: Feeling inferior. I think that I have more feelings about it now that I'm older than when I was younger. Maybe I'm more aware of it.

Interviewer: How did your parents handle this at the time?

Subject: They sent me to a psychologist. They say that teachers saw me as immature. Ya, I think my size and my maturity are linked there somehow.

Interviewer: Did you feel in high school that you were discounted because of your size?

Subject: After a while, with my experience of being in elementary school and going through a hell of a thing in Boston, you really buy into it. You buy into it that you are less—things aren't as expected of you as much.

Interviewer: What do you think the implications of "cute" have been for you?

Subject: Even though I know headwise that people say it in terms of a positive warm regard, I still view "cute" as being less than handsome or attractive. I just view it really negatively. I think it's a putdown.

Interviewer: What kind of sense of humor do you have?

Subject: I think my humor is very quick, very insightful, and it can be very sarcastic.

Interviewer: Then you went to college. How did you adapt?

Subject: I became very academically competitive. In class I was very verbal. I think when you are short, sometimes you don't get noticed. I think that is partly the reason for my being verbal.

Interviewer: How would life be different if you were taller?

Subject: People would view me as more competent. I believe I would feel better about myself.

Interviewer: What about your development: fourth to sixth grade, Little League?

Subject: I was the shortest on the team. I was discriminated against. I got the poorest positions.

Interviewer: Did height bother you?
Subject: When you are in a crowd, at a concert, and everybody stands up and you have to stand on a chair, it's embarrassing. A thought crosses my mind that I'm standing next to someone who is 1½ feet taller than me. I'm wondering what he thinks about me being this tall, and I feel like maybe there is an onus on me to prove that I am at least as intellectually worthy as a person.

Interviewer: Humor?
Subject: I kind of use humor like Judo or Aikido. If someone is making fun of me because of my height, I'll take it a step further than they did.

Interviewer: College: Is your experience of living or being different from others of average height?
Subject: The combination of being a student and being short made me feel like, well, when I was in a supervisory relationship, it made me feel like a kid. For me, the barrier is more in my own mind, that I felt younger 'cause I was smaller. When you are a head shorter than somebody, it is analogous to a child looking up at an adult. So I think, if anything, I still have to deal with the feeling of being littler. When I think of little, I think of younger.

Interviewer: Discrimination?
Subject: Last year when going for interviews, this guy had this couch that was about a foot too deep, and I felt that I either had to sit on the end or sit forward. I felt very small—like Alice in Wonderland or Tom Thumb. I walked out of there feeling very intimidated.

Interviewer: How do you deal with aggressive impulses?
Subject: My height protects me in some ways from physical aggression. It gives me some license to say things that I really feel without giving people a license to hit me.
Interviewer: How do you handle feelings of anger and aggression?
Subject: Sarcasm.
Interviewer: Has it always been that way?
Subject: That's been the main mode.

Interviewer: How did the family handle the fact that you were not going to grow up to be a strapping jock?
Subject: Mom was considering some sort of growth hormone drug. The version of the story that I remember was Dad talked her out of it.
Interviewer: Did you talk about it?
Subject: We talked about it. Mom's thought was that I would just have social problems, and she was anxious about that. She was constantly anxious about things that I had that would cause me social problems.
Interviewer: Does the use of humor play an important part in your life?
Subject: Most definitely. I use both extremes. I use it to tell people to get off my

case, and I also use it with people who I like very much and I'm comfortable with.

Based on an analysis of the interview data, certain conclusions may be drawn with reasonable confidence. There were some striking characteristics that were shared by most interview subjects. The interview data, seen in conjunction with both the previous literature and other facets of our research, support the possibility that a rather distinct personality constellation exists that characterizes many short males.

Identity and Humor

The short male experiences his height as his badge of identity. This badge of identity is negatively valenced and then cathected as an important aspect of his self-concept. Short stature, once internalized as part of his self-concept, becomes the core from which feelings of inferiority develop. Adolescence, a time when self-concept and body concept are heavily overlapping, is an especially difficult time for the short male. At this time he must confront his deficiency within the realms of competitive sports and heterosexual relationships. The outcome may be a denial of the importance of his body. The issues may be suppressed and repressed, but they remain unresolved and are carried into adulthood.

Certainly there are various subcategories of short males. Some short males are exceptionally athletic and/or attractive, and these individuals may come to terms with their short stature in ways that are different from the typical short male. The physically gifted short male may actually gain special attention because he is able to surprise people with his competence. However, within some athletic domains such as big-time college or professional football and basketball, evaluators tend to discount the small male's performance, sometimes acting as if it is temporary or accidental. Being precocious and gifted in other areas such as the arts and academics does not generally meet with such skepticism and can provide the short male with feelings of self-esteem that may transcend issues relating to his relative stature.

However, the great majority of short men must continually deal with the reality of their deficient stature. A typical coping pattern involves a relatively cerebral approach to life with a concurrent deemphasis on physical competence. The cerebral approach serves two functions: First, it allows the short male to develop a sense of self-worth that is not based exclusively on an inferior body. Second, it allows him to develop a new role that may be experienced in a predominantly conflict-free ego sphere. Overall, a cerebral approach is meant to serve an important equalizing function, while also protecting the individual from being overwhelmed by feelings of inferiority. By diminishing his emphasis on the importance of his body, the short male may be able to focus emotional and intellectual energy elsewhere, thereby making a satisfactory adult adjustment.

However, as disclosed in our clinical interviews, short men typically retain an underlying rage at having been "shortchanged." The derivative form of this rage is often manifested in sardonic humor whose main purpose is to express the underlying, perhaps unconscious, rage in an oblique manner. Short men tend to be acutely perceptive of defects and shortcomings in others. They can somehow cope with their deficiency in height if they can identify the flaws in their taller peers.

Humor allows for sparring with larger males while still remaining safe from physical harm. The short male will often have a rapier wit that allows him to get his point across while not risking the possibility of physical injury. As one interview subject noted: "My height protects me in some ways from physical aggression. It gives me some license to say things that I really feel without giving people a license to hit me." As the short male's physical safety may exist only at the whim of taller males, he cannot risk direct confrontation. To miss this essential point is to fail to understand the fundamental sizing up that exists in all interpersonal interactions. Even though the reality of being beaten up may cease to exist in the day-to-day social interactions of the middle-class male during the postadolescent period, he nevertheless has internalized his fear of physical vulnerability. As one interview subject succinctly stated: "Both he and I know if I go too far, he can always beat me up. This must have some effect on the way I act." It does seem to influence greatly the behavior of the short male by skewing his development enough to produce a relatively unique style.

Humor also serves to distract others from what the short male fears most: discussion of his short stature. As one interview subject revealed: "I kind of use humor like Judo or Aikido. If someone is making fun of me because of my height, I'll take it a step further than he did." This response is reminiscent of Cyrano de Bergerac, who outdoes those who mock him.

One potential adaptation, which depends on the use of humor, is the clowning or the mascot-adaptational response. The clowning response is learned early in the short male's life. This style represents an implicit contract between the short male and those with whom he comes in contact. Since the short male will rarely be admitted to the desirable peer group based on physical prowess, he must barter for entry with a different currency. As part of the contract, he agrees to serve as the mascot of the group. The price of this bargain is that the short male remains permanently uncertain of the centrality of his membership in the group and must always continue earning acceptance.

It is also relevant to mention that younger boys may develop a similar adaptational style in their attempt to become part of an older male peer group. Typically, younger boys are shorter than their older peers, and the connection between size and maturity level is clear-cut. Boys who are paternally deprived and seeking their identity through peer group activities, are especially prone to occupy a mascot-like position if they are also relatively young and/or small (Biller and Solomon 1986).

Impression Formation

The interview data point toward the conclusion that the short male is, indeed, likely to be insecure, but only within specified contexts. In these situations, the individual is in unfamiliar social territory with people whom he does not know very well. The social context brings into sharp focus the short male's relative stature. The interview subjects described these first meetings with others as the most difficult of tasks. They were acutely aware that, on first meetings, other people tend to think of them as less than or not as significant as. These meetings become a proving ground, a field for the experience of tension and anxiety, an arena for the display of their psychological defenses. As one interview subject responded to the question, "How would life be different for you if you were 5'10"?": "In general, in relations with people, there would be one less obstacle to overcome, or one less touchy subject to deal with in terms of meeting people."

In order to avoid attention to his height, the short male will, as another interview subject said, "present as standard a view of himself as possible." This fear of standing out (or rather standing beneath) represents a form of personal insecurity. It is as though, by not standing out, he believes that his short stature will not be noticed. Not to be perceived as short requires both a self-deception and a collusion that must exist between the short male and his taller counterparts. Both parties make an unspoken agreement not to mention the stature issue. Both agree to act as if there were no issue. Yet such an avoidance is not realistic or successful. As one interview subject noted: "I've always been insecure meeting new people just because I know that the first thing they are going to remark upon is my height."

Why is short stature somewhat different than other deviant physical characteristics? There is a surprisingly simple answer to this question. The important difference is that stature taps psychological conditioning felt by all and directly acknowledged by almost none. The discomfort in dealing with inappropriate relative stature is visible only in the joking comment and nervous laughter. For example, if we were to look at the problem as an issue of discrimination, most people would rarely admit that they are actively discriminating against an individual because of his short stature. Moreover, even if they have a basic prejudice concerning short men, they may not be aware of it. In fact, the short male himself, for psychodynamic reasons, may not view himself as being discriminated against. To acknowledge discrimination, he would have to think of himself as having a disability, and he may not be prepared to make such an admission. In any event, the issue is rarely handled in a direct manner.

As a result of this pervasive reluctance of either party to acknowledge the issue, the short male is likely to receive much inaccurate feedback from the interpersonal environment, making it impossible for him to develop a realistic understanding of the impact of his short stature. He is, thus, left to construct his own idiosyncratic understanding of his impact on people around him. This may

lead to the paranoid position of which short males are often accused. For example, one short male (5'3") asked his father why he was so short. His father
replied, "Oh, you're not so short." This exchange highlights one of the essential
problems. The short male experiences thoughts and feelings in response to subtle
and covert cues from the environment; however, for the reasons already mentioned, many of those he interacts with negate the legitimacy of the concerns.
It is, as Keyes (1980) notes, like "fighting a ghost." The paranoid position may
be too harsh a term, but what it is meant to communicate is the acute oversen-
sitivity to personal slight that often develops as the short male attempts to understand what is so wrong with him that he generates such uncomfortable reactions in others.

The short male is often poised waiting for hints of personal slight. Since he
usually will not respond to such suggestions of personal slight directly, the ac-
curacy of his perception of being discriminated against is rarely verified in a
direct manner. What can result is interpersonal cautiousness, coupled with the
appearance of gregariousness. The short male may enjoy being with his fellow
men, while understanding, on some level, that he is not fully accepted as a member of the group. Although the experienced difference is not often openly articulated, it has a profound impact on the way the short male feels about himself
vis-à-vis his contemporaries.

Adult Insecurity

The short male's difficulties in gaining peer acceptance and feeling part of a male
group is a persistent and continuing developmental problem. As long as relationships remain on a mature, distant, adult basis, few problems are experienced.
When, however, a certain level of closeness is achieved, the relationship may
begin to take on more adolescent qualities, becoming reminiscent of the short
male's relationships when he was younger. This is a distinctive feature of the
short male's disability: When he is involved in a close relationship, regression is
likely to occur which places him in the role of a child or adolescent, making him
vulnerable to becoming the powerless person in the relationship. The short male
does try to convince himself that that was then and this is now, but there are
casual references to his height that serve as powerful reminders. People who are
treating him familiarly will frequently refer to his height as his distinguishing
characteristic, often doing so in a joking manner so that direct confrontation
by him becomes inappropriate.

As a likely result of others' reactions when intimacy develops, the short male
will keep a habitual emotional distance in interpersonal situations, that is, he
will interact with others in a relatively superficial way through humor and con-
versational skills, while also using these resources as a means of warding off true
intimacy. Hence, there will remain a highly sensitive core of insecurity, hidden

rage, and loneliness based on a deeply experienced knowledge of being different. The possibility of disconfirming experiences of healthy intimacy and acceptance is reduced further by the short male's use of distance as a defense. Over time, many short males develop a personality that is seen by others as personable but somewhat aloof and self-contained. Since the short male does want to be a part of the larger males' peer group, he often appears willing to accept his role as either mascot or intellectual contributor.

None of the interview subjects admitted seeking support from other short males. In fact, the distinct impression was that short males tend to avoid contact with one another. They seem to want to avoid the possibility that others would think they were grouping themselves based on height, which would be a social acknowledgement by them of their stature difference. Although the potential for increased group power and the development of positive self-regard is available, it has not been seized upon. While some other minorities have powerful support and advocacy groups, the short male acts as if the issues are not present. Although lack of cohesiveness is a common problem of low-status groups, the short male thereby forfeits an opportunity to identify positively with a peer group that might be especially significant for him. (It is relevant to mention that there have been some organizing activities among extremely short and physically handicapped individuals such as dwarfs or midgets, but men between 5'2" and 5'5" clearly are not part of this group. See Ablon 1984.)

Since short height is often associated with being childlike and in a subordinate relationship, the major question facing the short male as an adult is how to manage the incongruity between his adult self-image and his treatment as a child in a way that allows for self-respect, good relations with others, and the maintenance of a sense of competence. The re-emergence of earlier developmental issues is an ongoing problem for the short male that is especially poignant. Even as an adult, the short male must endure joking comments about his shortness. These potentially difficult situations are often handled by the short male with humor and diplomacy, but their impact on him is to remind him frequently that, no matter how old, established, or successful he becomes, he will always be subject to this form of abuse. It allows those joking with him to put him in his place—a place that is socially inferior to theirs; thus, the threat of such encounters persists. For these reasons, the short male may be wary of new relationships or increasing closeness in a relationship because such situations bring with them the potential for the re-emergence of unwanted feelings and troublesome interpersonal issues.

Overall, results of the interview study suggest that short stature in middle-class Caucasian males may lead to the adoption of a distinct and identifiable defensive style. As the result of a sense of body inferiority and vulnerability, short males may rely excessively on rational and analytic skills to the relative exclusion of physical and social skills. Paralleling the development of a cerebral approach is the denial of the importance of the body. The underlying anger at being discriminated against and made to feel inferior often surfaces, in part, as a sarcastic sense of humor.

Interacting Factors

While middle class males depend more heavily on intellectual abilities and humor, such attributes may not be valued as highly in different socioeconomic and sociocultural environments. The short male who lives in a lower socioeconomic environment or is of an ethnic group that places a high value on machismo, will very likely develop a different adaptation to his short stature. Within his environment, the cerebral approach might only bring derision and exclusion from his peers. In fact, it might threaten his very survival unless, of course, he is able to move away to another, more middle-class environment.

As a result, we might speculate that the adaptation of the lower-class short male might often take the form of exaggerated machismo, the purpose of which is to prove to himself and to others that he is as much a man as anyone else. In this environment, the short male would have to establish his place quickly within his peer group to avoid frequent challenges because of his short stature. However, no research on the topic of short stature in males has systematically addressed socioeconomic or ethnic differences.

Physical prowess is an especially central value defining masculinity in lower socioeconomic groups. Our observations suggest that a higher proportion of short lower-class males, as compared to middle-class males, adopt a tough guy, daredevil, or Don Juan style of adaptation. Some of these short males achieve a successful physically based adaptation, but most continue to suffer from feelings of inferiority, particularly if they do not have a relatively mesomorphic body build. On the other hand, it appears that short males are much more likely to attain a positive level of self-acceptance if they grow up in a middle-class environment, in which there is an emphasis on intellectual and artistic accomplishment.

As emphasized in chapter 3, developmental stage issues can be very important for the individual in coming to grips with his short stature. Early maturing generally is associated with long-term advantages for the male. However, there is a subgroup of early maturers whose advantage is quite temporary because they remain relatively short while most of their peers catch up and surpass them in physical development. They have to give up what appeared to be a superior physical status by midadolescence. Their initial athletic and social success may be quite short-lived unless they are physically gifted enough to compensate for their short stature. Their self-concepts may be especially threatened if they do not have other areas of competence which distinguish them from their peers.

Another potentially interesting area for further research would be a study in which the experience of older adult short males is systematically examined. We might hypothesize that the impact of short stature on a male would reach a peak in late adolescence and decrease in importance as he matures. Once he has found a spouse, achieved professional success, and developed his self-esteem, we could reasonably expect that the salience of the height issue would dissipate. Whether or not a short male copes adequately with the height issue is related to intervening variables, such as family support, his intellectual gifts, and his socioeconomic environment. The results of the present investigation indicate that both additional research and a greater sensitivity to interacting factors are needed.

The way in which a particular short male copes with a relative stature disadvantage depends on the interaction of constitutional, social, and family influences. It is important to emphasize that short males who are disadvantaged in areas in addition to their stature are especially at risk to experience severe self-concept problems. Being short and having a nonmesomorphic physique, being short and having intellectual limitations and/or an unsupportive family environment greatly increase the individual's vulnerability. Short stature can be viewed as a disability in the same general way that a specific learning disorder might be viewed. Given appropriate resources, an individual can usually cope with it over time, but given other limitations, his feelings of self-worth are likely to be severely and irrevocably damaged (Biller and Solomon 1986).

On the other hand, the developmental outcome is likely to be quite positive when the short male has the advantage of an otherwise well-developed physique, above-average intellectual potential, a supportive family, and opportunities provided by an upper-middle-class socioeconomic background. Nevertheless, no matter how successful they may eventually be, there are very few, if any, short men who do not experience significant stress as they have to cope developmentally with the reality of their stature deficiency.

Results from the interview study underscored the potential interaction between a highly supportive family environment and successful adaptation and coping. The degree to which parents are able to be accepting of their short sons has considerable influence on their level of psychological functioning. As Gillis (1982) pointed out, for example: "An adolescent boy, who is fundamentally secure and has warm accepting parents and generally rewarding social relationships, may not develop strong feelings of inadequacy even if he matures slowly" (p. 253). Gillis goes on to say, "Talking with many well-adjusted short and tall people, I have found that the most common reason they give to explain their successful adaptation is the support they received from their parents" (p. 193).

Family environment forms the basis for the successful development of self-esteem and interpersonal competence. The development of emotional security within the family may serve to inoculate the short boy from difficulties in the larger social arena. If a solid sense of self-worth has been fostered within the family, the assaults to self-esteem can be significantly minimized although not full eradicated. In contrast, the combination of an unsupportive family environment and a larger social environment insensitive to his needs places the short boy at great risk for the development of emotional problems.

The short boy (or the boy with an unmasculine physique) seems especially vulnerable when he also suffers from paternal deprivation, including various forms of the father's absence from the home and inadequate or neglectful fathering (Biller and Solomon 1986). The boy who feels a lack of peer acceptance is in special need of the emotional support of an involved father (or effective father-substitute) if he is to develop a healthy sense of self-worth.

The child's adjustment to being short is also related to his relative stature within the family. A boy whose father or brother is short is likely to be more accepting of himself than is the boy who is much shorter than other males in

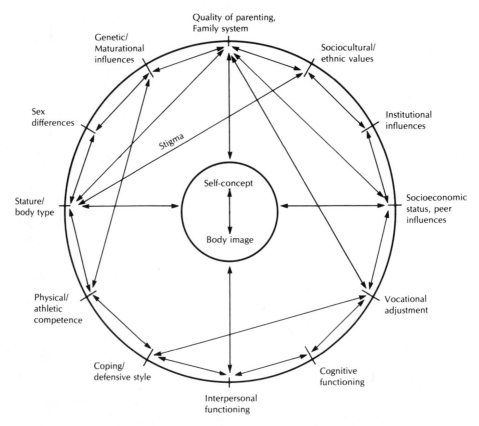

**Figure 6–1. Preliminary Outline of Transactional Model Relating
Stature to Self-concept and Psychosocial Development**

his family. A particularly difficult situation for the short boy is to have a younger brother who is taller than himself. Some of our interview subjects reported especially intense conflicts and anger concerning the presence of a taller and stronger younger male sibling in their family. On the other hand, short males who were only children or the only boys in their families seemed more likely to experience an earlier self-acceptance, especially if their fathers were also short.

Having a short child may be particularly unsettling for parents who do not have a family history of short stature. For example, the father who is 5'5" may be more accepting of his relatively short son than the father who is 6'2". The tall father may also continually expect his son to suddenly grow and be likely to blame the child, or someone else, when this does not happen. As might be expected, however, many short fathers feel very ambivalent toward their short sons. Fathers who have not achieved a positive body image themselves may be especially threatened when they have a son who is relatively small for his age.

Attribution of Personality Traits

The prediction was strongly supported that the sample as a whole would attribute more negatively valenced and less socially valued personality traits and personal qualities to men of short height than to men of either average or tall height. On the Semantic Differential Measure, men of tall and average height were seen as significantly more mature, uninhibited, positive, secure, masculine, active, complete, successful, optimistic, dominant, capable, confident, and outgoing than men of short height.

When the data were analyzed along the Evaluation, Potency, and Activity factors, analogous results were found. On the Evaluation factor, men of short height were seen less favorably than either of the other two groups. On the Potency factor, significant differences between all three height designations were found, with men of short height seen as least potent, and men of tall height seen as most potent. On the Activity factor, significant differences between all three height designations were also found, with men of tall height seen as most active, and men of short height seen as least active.

Essentially, regardless of their own height, the subjects attributed less favorable characteristics to men of short height. The short subjects viewed themselves less favorably, revealing something about their self-concept. The attitudes toward short males were negatively valenced. These views were, to some extent, internalized by the short male, becoming part of their self-concepts. In contrast, the group attributed positively valenced characteristics to men of tall height, and the tall subjects were very positively cathected to their own height. These results are consistent with literature reviewed in chapters 1 through 4.

If we accept the viewpoint that an individual's genetically determined attributes interact with social learning variables in subtle ways, it becomes clear why short stature has important implications for personality development. In Western society, tall stature and a mesomorphic body type in males brings esteem and facilitates the acquisition of rewarding resources. The short male's failure to, at least, approximate the cultural ideal for height results in his being the recipient of lesser social power, lower perceptual impact or "presence," and decreased desirability as a heterosexual partner. Although the admiration for large size in males may have survival value in pretechnological cultures, it seems no longer directly relevant to our society's goals or a means of adaptation. However, over time the seemingly instinctive social preference for big males profoundly influences an individual's social learning history. Boys who are short will be less likely as a group to achieve success in obtaining positive reinforcement from their peers. This may lead to a "flight from the body world" (Fisher 1973) or a movement toward more intellectual pursuits.

Social learning theory would suggest that individuals will behave in a manner consistent with the expectations of others. If, as Staffieri (1967) points out, the expectations regarding body types are consistent and long-lasting, behavior will conform to such expectations. Ultimately, one does not end up with a self-fulfilling prophecy but rather a social-fulfilling prophecy (McCandless 1960). The male who is consistently treated as inferior because he is short gradually internalizes a very negative image of himself.

While no systematic research has been conducted, one potential coping behavior for the stresses of short male stature in adolescence is the choice of homosexuality as a sexual orientation. This allows avoidance of heterosexual competition and accommodates the short boy's admiration for height in taller males. Although this choice of lifestyle does not meet with general societal acceptance, it brings membership in a male group that may provide a strong sense of belonging which the short boy might not otherwise experience.

The authors' strong clinical impression is that more short boys than tall boys encounter developmental difficulties associated with emotional, social, and sex role problems. Our experience suggests that a greater proportion of short boys are involved in counseling, psychotherapy, or some form of family treatment. How much this reflects an actual difference in psychological adjustment, or how much this is a reflection of parental concerns is open to question. However, it does appear that, other things being equal, short boys seem to encounter more developmental conflicts with parents, siblings, and peers.

Medical Advances and Parenting Issues

The U.S. Food and Drug Administration has approved the use of a genetically engineered (synthetic) human growth hormone (Gertner 1986). Demand for growth hormone treatment by parents is expected to be overwhelming, even though the treatment is painful and potentially dangerous.

Given this technological advance, it becomes imperative for both medical and mental health professionals to develop a better understanding of the potential developmental issues concerning short stature. Parents who communicate their own anxiety over height may be planting the seeds of emotional difficulties. The issue needs to be handled sensitively, with an appreciation for the possibility that the risks of hormone therapy may outweigh the potential gains. Parents may need counseling about the best way to address these issues with their child.

The study of children with growth deficiencies has led to some provocative observations. To some extent, many of the issues parallel those in families with a handicapped or medically disabled child (Rotnam 1984). Parents in such families typically share an especially pervasive uncertainty concerning their child's future development. When the child's growth is perceived as very discrepant with his chronological age, parents are more likely to feel guilty and to be overprotective or overrestrictive. Parents are apt to be intensely concerned that the child is vulnerable to hurt by insensitive peers, and may discourage the child from being socially assertive (Rotnam, Cohen, Hintz, and Genel, 1979; Rotnam, Genel, Hintz, and Cohen, 1977).

Diagnosis

Even if other medical handicaps are not involved, parents generally have a very difficult time accepting a diagnosis that their child will remain much shorter than average. The medical and mental health professional may expect the parents to be greatly relieved to hear that their child is completely healthy (though destined to be relatively short). However, they can also expect much parental defensiveness in reaction to an otherwise benign diagnosis. Accepting a generally healthy but chronically short son may be especially difficult for fathers. On the other hand, when the stature deficiency is diagnosed as part of serious medical problems, parents are still likely to be highly defensive about accepting that their child will remain relatively short. The intensity of parental feelings regarding the size of their child is something that health care professionals need to deal with in a sensitive and supportive manner (Rotnam 1984).

The diagnosis of the specific etiological conditions underlying some cases of short stature can be a complex process requiring a thorough endocrinological workup. Many cases of short stature are associated with other obvious medical and/or developmental problems, including cognitive and neuromuscular deficits. However, some of the most difficult parental and pediatric decisions involve children who are significantly shorter than average but otherwise seem to be developing quite normally with respect to basic cognitive and physical functions.

It is important to point out again that the short subjects in our sample did not have any clearcut medical or endocrinological problems (Martel and Biller 1986). According to our interview data, most of their parents seemed concerned that their sons were below average in stature and some consulted medical specialists. However, there was usually a grudging acceptance that their child had "short genes," mixed with the frequent hope that during later adolescence he might have a growth spurt. In any case, although not without typical conflicts, most of our subjects indicated that they grew up in generally supportive and accepting family environments.

It is essential for parents to do some medical reality testing if they are concerned about their children's stature. By the elementary school years, the short child is likely to be at least somewhat anxious about being smaller than his peers. From a clinical perspective, if the child is healthy and is growing (even if at a somewhat slower rate than average), supportive parent and family counseling rather than further biomedical intervention may be the most meaningful approach. Of course, any indications of endrocrinological abnormalities should be thoroughly investigated (Gertner 1986). Interestingly, there has been some research comparing the adjustments of short statured children with and without endocrine deficiencies. Steinhausen and Stahnke (1976) concluded that personality development in very short children is much more a function of having to cope with relatively short stature than of whether or not they have specific endocrine deficiencies. They found that parental responses to their short children did not differ based on whether the stature deficit was or was not endocrinologically based.

From a developmental perspective, the age at which a child begins to be perceived as smaller than average by parents may be quite important. It is usually somewhat easier for parents to inhibit their excessively protective tendencies if their child has a solid developmental history of achievement before they perceive that he has a stature deficiency. The child whose shortness only becomes apparent when he is seven or eight or older may be in a much different situation than the child who was very small even as a preschooler. The older child has had the opportunity to develop sufficient competency to at least to some extent counteract overprotective parental attitudes, whereas the infant and toddler is more likely to be the recipient of excessive anxiety and concern.

The child who is very small for his age needs to receive parental acceptance and support to develop his potential. Well-meaning parents sometimes go to an extreme and overencourage the small child to engage in nonphysical activities and/or to avoid competitive sports. If a child is frustrated by group athletics, however, he may enjoy, for example, gymnastics, certain track events, or tennis. There are many athletic experiences that can aid in the development of body image and a strong sense of physical competence, without unduly putting the small individual at a disadvantage.

Despite his short stature, parents should help the child to develop as positive a body image as possible. Assuming the child is responsive, physical fitness activities, even at a very early age, can be quite important. As the young boy gets older, weight-lifting and/or Nautilus programs can also be constructive in physical development. In *Father Power*, Biller and Meredith (1974) offer many relevant suggestions for parents in encouraging their children's physical development, including ways in which fathers and mothers can also benefit with respect to their own sense of well-being, health, and fitness. Father-and-son physical and athletic activities (as well as intellectual activities) which emphasize mutual enjoyment may be especially important for the short boy (or the boy who has an unmasculine physique) as a way of lessening the risks of a poor body image and/ or preventing a flight from the body world.

Clinicians who treat individuals and families should also be aware of the impact of short stature in males. A general bias within the field of mental health is to minimize the importance of the body as a determinant of emotional well-being. Clinicians, when treating the short boy (and even the short adult male), should inquire sensitively as to the impact of short stature on his development. Both the parents' and the child's views may yield valuable information about the child's functioning. An inquiry into the importance and impact of short stature may be particularly significant if the child is having problems in school and/or emotional difficulties.

At present, no generally applicable guidelines exist for the clinical assessment of the impact of short stature. It is hoped, however, that the types of questions asked in our interview study (see pages 82–87) may have heuristic value in developing a more comprehensive approach. Future research goals should include the development of such assessment guidelines. At the least, during the clinical evaluation the individual's subjective feelings regarding his height and other physical attributes should be assessed along with a measurement of his physical size with regard to published norms for his age group. A boy, for example, who is more than one standard deviation below the average height for his age is certainly at risk for psychological difficulties. It is essential to begin making others, including parents and educators, aware of this important issue so that the building blocks of self-esteem for the short boy may be more solidly constructed.

The Other Side

It would be a disservice to focus only on the disadvantages associated with short stature. Being short may indeed be viewed as a significant risk factor as it relates to personality development, but one must be aware of the fact that people with a "disability" do not necessarily become disabled.

There may in fact be some developmental benefits that accrue from the successful negotiation of the "disability." Being faced with and surmounting difficult issues during development may serve to build and enhance character strengths. The short male may develop much interpersonal sensitivity and sharp analytic skills. On the other hand, there may be some eventual costs for tall mesomorphic males whose physical attributes make it extremely easy for them to be socially and athletically successful as children and as adolescents. Some tall well-built males may have no incentive to develop their intellectual potential or learn how to cope with adversity, and, thus, may have a very difficult time dealing with the inevitable stresses of adulthood. The on-going process of successfully coping with adversity increases one's sense of self-confidence, self-efficacy, and personal empowerment. Ultimately, the "successful" short male may possess a combination of resources that includes interpersonal sensitivity and excellent intellectual and diplomacy skills, as well as a higher than average drive toward continued achievement.

Research and clinical impression suggest that there is a developmental push for the short middle-class male toward the artistic-intellectual sphere of achievement. Upon examination, this appears to be a "logical" solution to a difficult developmental dilemma. A positive male identity and self-image must be forged, and it almost certainly cannot be done through the traditional masculine routes. The artistic-intellectual domains do not require height as an admission criterion.

In the light of medical technology's increasing ability to engineer human genetic material, individual differences in height (and other physical characteristics) may potentially be significantly diminished. Nevertheless, the ability to tolerate differences is a mark of a mature society. As the farthest deviations from the social ideals of physical characteristics are eliminated, the range of acceptable normality will no doubt contract. Because of this concern, the positive aspects of difference also require more careful investigation.

Further Considerations

Behavioral researchers must begin to integrate biological realities more seriously into their psychosocial explanations of human development. It is disheartening how the important contributions of such great scientists as Gesell and Sheldon have often been minimized or brushed aside because their biological and maturational orientations did not fit with the more popular contemporary environmentalist Zeitgeist. With respect to our focus, it is noteworthy that individual differences in height and body type have been found to be consistently related to many different aspects of psychological and social functioning. Body appearance factors, in general, are at least as significant as child-rearing and cultural factors in determining the individual's self-concept and social success. Obviously, there is an interaction between biological and sociocultural factors, but to try to simply explain the former as a function of the latter is to deny biosocial realities.

An important clinical and educational implication is that there be an honest confrontation of cultural stereotypes relating to stature and other dimensions of physical appearance. The denial that such stereotypes exist, or the pretension that they do not have a powerful psychological impact, is counterproductive. We should not be afraid to admit their pervasive existence. Part of parent training and teacher training, as well as affective education for children in schools, should include an examination of stereotypes about stature and body type in a way that highlights their existence but also cautions against generalizing their meaningfulness to the self and to others. Biological realities and individual differences must be considered along with discriminatory stereotypes.

Parents, teachers, and employers should become more aware of their own potentially discriminatory attitudes toward short males and should be very careful to make sure that their judgements are based on behavioral information rather than on knee-jerk stereotypes. A child should not be discouraged from performing a particular activity if he is interested, but he should also be prepared for the possibility that others may prejudge his motivation and/or competence. In this way, with the support of significant others, the child may develop the confidence to surmount social obstacles, assuming he has the basic competence. Whether the child is striving for respect for his opinions, social acceptance, a leadership role, or a position on an athletic team, assertiveness in countering stereotypes is quite important. In many ways, the issues are quite similar to those confronting individuals who face discrimination because of their racial or sociocultural identification.

Much of the style of interpersonal relationships—especially the traditional expectations that men should be more assertive, aggressive, and dominant in dating, courtship, and leadership situations—although subject to cultural variation is to some extent based on the biological reality of sexual dimorphism, with males typically being significantly larger than females at least by late adolescence. Relatively short stature is more often a generalized psychosocial handicap for men than for women. Being short and petite is typically viewed as a positive feminine characteristic, so that for a woman it may be an asset in many aspects of social development. Nonetheless, the short female may share *some* of the same difficulties confronting the short male. Because of her lack of stature, she may be perceived as immature and childlike, and perhaps more importantly as she reaches adolescence she may find it difficult to directly influence others' opinions and decisions. On the other hand, although the very tall or large female may be at a disadvantage because she is not viewed as positively feminine, her size no doubt gives her some potential advantage with regard to social influence and leadership. Other things being equal, similar to the small male, the small female is much more likely to be intimidated or physically taken advantage of than are her taller and bigger peers.

A compelling research implication that may be drawn from the present volume is that investigators interested in the impact of family and social variables on personality development should include at least a simple assessment of stature and body type in their data analyses. A simple direct measurement of height and body type, or a question that asks subjects to estimate their height and body type could make research on the family and the child more meaningful. Even though there is some evidence that very short subjects might overestimate their actual height by an inch or so, such a simple questionnaire measure is extremely reliable relative to other types of attitude and value assessments.

For the same basic reasons, the clinician interested in doing a personality assessment should also take the time to determine the client's relative height, weight, body type, and other characteristics related to physical appearance, as well as how the client compares to other family members and significant others with respect to these factors. Every clinician working with children, for example, should have up-to-date tables concerning age-related height and weight norms, and percentiles.

Some researchers certainly should seek out more basic physical indexes (e.g., skeletal age, hormonal balance, etc.) in exploring biological factors that influence complex human behavior. However, even more superficial measures of factors that are relatively impervious to variations in child-rearing (except with extreme maltreatment), such as stature, body type, and temperament, can provide insights into the complex processes of personality development. We need to ask more specific questions such as: "What types of child-rearing and peer group patterns are most conducive to the development of a positive self-concept and social competence for boys who are short and/or nonmesomorphic in body type?"

It is ironic that there seems to have been, at least proportionately, more research in the 1950s and 1960s that at least included both child-rearing and body type measures than in the 1970s and 1980s (e.g., Biller 1968, Mussen and Jones, 1957, Washburn 1962). We hope that the present volume will, at least, make a small contribution to raising the consciousness of researchers and clinicians to the interacting effect of biological, family system, and social factors in psychological functioning and personality development.

References

Ablon, J. (1984). *Little people in America: The social dimensions of dwarfism.* New York: Praeger Publishers.

Abraham, S., Johnson, C., and Najjar, M. (1979). *Weight and height of adults 18–74 years of age: United States 1971–1974.* Hyattsville, MD: U.S. Department of Health, Education, and Welfare.

Adams, R. (1980). Social psychology and beauty: Effects of age, height, and weight on self reported personality traits and social behavior. *Journal of Social Psychology, 112,* 287–293.

Adler, A. (1956). *The individual psychology of Alfred Adler.* New York: Basic Books.

Albaum, G., Best, R., and Hawkins, D. (1981). Continuous vs. discrete semantic differential scales. *Psychological Reports, 49,* 83–86.

Ames, R. (1957). Physical maturing among boys as related to adult social behavior: A longitudinal study. *California Journal of Educational Research, 8,* 69–75.

Arkoff, A. and Weaver, B. (1966). Body image and body dissatisfaction in Japanese Americans. *Journal of Social Psychology, 68,* 323–330.

Bailey, K.G. (1976). Body size as implied threat: Effects on personal perception. *Perceptual and Motor Skills, 43,* 223–230.

Baker, E.E. and Redding, W.C. (1961). The effect of perceived tallness in persuasive speaking: An experiment. *Journal of Communication Studies, 12,* 51.

Baldwin, B.J. (1921). Physical growth of children from birth to maturity. *University of Iowa Studies, 1.*

Bandura, A. and Walters, R. (1963). *Social learning and personality development.* New York: Holt, Rinehart, and Winston.

Barker, R.G. (1953). *A survey of the social psychology of physique and disability.* New York: Social Science Research Council.

Barker, R.G., Wright, B.A., and Gonick, M.R. (1946). *Adjustment to physical handicap and illness: A survey of the social psychology of physique and disability.* New York: Social Science Research Council.

Beigel, H. (1954). Body height in mate selection. *Journal of Social Psychology, 29,* 257–268.

Berkowitz, W. (1969). Perceived height, personality and friendship choice. *Psychological Reports, 24,* 373–374.

Berlinsky, E.B. and Biller, H.B. (1982). *Parental death and psychological development.* Lexington, MA: Lexington Books, D.C. Heath & Company.

Berscheid, E. and Walster, E. (1972). Beauty and the best. *Psychology Today*, 5(10), 42–46.

Berscheid, E. and Walster, E. (1974). Physical attractiveness. *Advances in Experimental Social Psychology.* Vol. 7, New York: Academic Press.

Berscheid, E., Walster, E., and Bohrnstedt, G. (1972). Body image: a Psychology Today questionnaire. *Psychology Today*, 6(2), 57–66.

Berscheid, E., Walster, E., and Bohrnstedt, G. (1973). The happy American body, a survey report. *Psychology Today*, 7(6), 119–146.

Best, J. (1977). *Research in education.* Englewood Cliffs, NJ: Prentice-Hall.

Biller, H.B. (1968). A multiaspect investigation of masculine development in kindergarten-age boys. *Genetic Psychology Monographs*, 76, 89–139.

Biller, H.B. (1971). *Father, child, and sex role.* Lexington, MA: Lexington Books, D.C. Heath & Company.

Biller, H.B. (1974). *Paternal deprivation: Family, school, sexuality and society.* Lexington, MA: Lexington Books, D.C. Heath & Company.

Biller, H.B. and Borstelmann, L.J. (1967). Masculine development: An integrative review. *Merrill-Palmer Quarterly*, 13, 253–294.

Biller, H.B. and Liebman, D.A. (1971). Body build, sex-role preference and sex-role adoption in junior high school boys. *Journal of Genetic Psychology*, 118, 81–86.

Biller, H.B. and Meredith, D.L. (1974). *Father power.* New York: David McKay. Reprinted, New York: Doubleday Anchor Books, 1975.

Biller, H.B. and Solomon, R.S. (1986). *Child maltreatment and paternal deprivation: A manifesto for research, prevention and treatment.* Lexington, MA: Lexington Books, D.C. Heath & Company.

Bolcraft, R. and Simmons, R.G. (1981). The impact of puberty on adolescents: A longitudinal study. Paper presented at the annual meeting of the American Psychological Association, Los Angeles, CA, August.

Brackbill, Y. and Nevill, D. (1981). Parental expectations of achievement as affected by children's height. *Merrill-Palmer Quarterly*, 27(4), 429–441.

Brodsky, C.M. (1954). *A study of norms for body form-behavior relationships.* Washington, DC: Catholic University of America Press.

Brunswik, E. (1956). *Perception and the representative design of psychological experiments.* Berkeley: University of California Press.

Calden, G., Lundy, R.M., and Schlafer, R.J. (1959). Sex differences in body concepts. *Journal of Consulting Psychology*, 23, 378.

Caplan, M.E. and Goldman, M. (1981). Personal space violations as a function of height. *Journal of Social Psychology*, 114(2), 167–171.

Carson, R. (1969). *Interaction concepts of personality.* Chicago: Aldine Publishing Co.

Chumelly, W.C. (1982). Physical growth in adolescence. In B.B. Wolman (ed.), *Handbook of developmental psychology.* Englewood Cliffs, NJ: Prentice-Hall, 471–485.

Clarke, W.V. (1956). The construction of an industrial selection personality test. *Journal of Psychology*, 41, 379–394.

Cobb, H.V. (1954). Role wishes and general wishes of children and adolescents. *Child Development*, 60, 392–400.

Conroy, P. (1976). *The Great Santini.* Boston: Houghton-Mifflin.

Cortés, J.B. and Gatti, F.M. (1965). Physique and self-description of temperament. *Journal of Consulting Psychology*, 29, 432–439.

Coyne, L. and Holzman, P. (1966). Three equivalent forms of a semantic differential inventory. *Educational and Psychological Measurement, 26,* 665–674.

Cronbach, L.J. (1951). Coefficient alpha and the internal structure of tests. *Psychometrika, 16,* 297–334.

Dannenmaier, H. and Thumin, F.J. (1964). Authority status as a factor in perceptual distortion of size. *Journal of Social Psychology, 63,* 361.

Darden, E. (1972). A comparison of body image and self-concept variables among various sport groups. *Research Quarterly, 43*(1), 7–15.

Deck, L. (1971). Short workers of the world unite. *Psychology Today, 5,* 102.

Dion, K.F. and Berscheid, E. (1974). Physical attractiveness and peer acceptance among children. *Sociometry, 37,* 1–2.

Dion, K.F., Berscheid, E., and Walster, E. (1972). What is beautiful is good. *Journal of Personality and Social Psychology, 24,* 285–290.

Divesta, F. and Walls, R. (1970). Factor analysis of the semantic attributes of 487 words and some relationships to the conceptual behavior of fifth grade children. *Journal of Educational Psychology Monograph, 61*(6), part 2.

Dixon, W.J. (1981). BMDP4V statistical software. Berkeley: University of California Press.

Dwyer, J. and Mayer, J. (1968). Psychological effects of variations in physical appearance during adolescence. *Adolescence, 3,* 353–380.

Eisenberg, N., Roth, K., Bryniarski, K.A., and Murray, E. (1984). Sex differences in the relationship of height to children's actual and attributed social and cognitive competencies. *Sex Roles, 11,* 719–734.

Eisenberg, P. (1937). Factors related to feelings of dominance. *Journal of Consulting Psychology, 1,* 89–92.

Elman, D. (1977). Physical characteristics and the perception of masculine traits. *Journal of Social Psychology, 103,* 157.

Erikson, E. (1963). *Childhood and society.* New York: W.W. Norton.

Feldman, S.D. (1975). The presentation of shortness in everyday life—height and heightism in American society. In *Lifestyles: Diversity in American society.* Boston: Little, Brown & Company.

Fenichel, O. (1945). *The psychoanalytic theory of neurosis.* New York: W.W. Norton and Co.

Finch, E. (1978). Clinical assessment of short stature. Unpublished medical school thesis, Yale University.

Finley, B.S., Crouthamel, C.S., and Richmond, R.A. (1981). A psychosocial intervention program for children with short stature and their families. *Social Work in Health Care, 7*(1), 27–34.

Fisher, S. (1964). Power orientation and concepts of self-height in men: Preliminary data. *Perceptual and Motor Skills, 18,* 737.

Fisher, S. (1965). Body image and psychopathology. *Research of Genetic Psychiatry, 10,* 519–529.

Fisher, S. (1970). *Body experience in fantasy and behavior.* New York: Appleton-Century-Crofts.

Fisher, S. (1973). *Body consciousness: You are what you feel.* Englewood Cliffs, NJ: Prentice-Hall, Inc.

Fisher, S., and Cleveland, S. (1968). *Body image and personality.* New York: Dover Publishers.

Fleming, I. (1959). *Goldfinger.* New York: Macmillan Press.

Freud, S. (1924). *Collected Papers.* London: The Hogarth Press.

Ford, C.S. and Beach, F.A. (1951). *Patterns of sexual behavior.* New York: Harper & Row.

Galbraith, J.K. (1977). Interview in *The Christian Science Monitor, 159,* May 18, p. 22.

Garai, J.E. and Scheinfeld, A. (1968). Sex differences in mental and behavioral traits. *Genetic Psychology Monographs, 77,* 169–269.

Gardner, L.I. (1972). Deprivation dwarfism. *Scientific American, 227,* 76–82.

Gascaly, A. and Borges, C.A. (1979). The male physique and behavioral experience expectancies. *Journal of Psychology, 106*(1), 97–102.

Gates, A.I. (1924). The nature and educational significance of physical status and of mental, physiological, social, and emotional maturity. *Journal of Educational Psychology, 15,* 329–358.

Gershon, M. and Biller, H.B. (1977). *The other helpers: Paraprofessionals and nonprofessionals in mental health.* Lexington, MA: Lexington Books.

Gertner, J.M. (1986). Short stature in children. *Medical Aspects of Human Sexuality, 20*(8), 36–42.

Gesell, A. (1928). *Infancy and human growth.* New York: Macmillan.

Gillis, J.S. (1982). *Too tall too small.* Champagne, IL: Institute for Personality and Ability Testing.

Gillis, J.S. and Avis, W.E. (1980). The male-taller norm in mate selection. *Personality and Social Psychology Bulletin, 6*(3), 396–401.

Glueck, S. and Glueck, E. (1956). *Physique and delinquency.* New York: Harper and Row.

Goffman, E. (1963). *Stigma.* Englewood Cliffs, NJ: Prentice-Hall.

Goldberg, B. and Folkins, C. (1974). Relationship of body image to negative emotional attitudes. *Perceptual and Motor Skills, 39*(3), 1053–1054.

Graziano, W. et al. (1978). Height and attraction: Do men see women eye to eye? *Journal of Personality, 46,* 128–145.

Green, A.A. (1983). Method for earlier recognition of abnormal stature. *Archives of Diseases of Childhood, 58*(7), 535–537.

Grew, R., Stabler, B., Williams, R., and Underwood, L.E. (1983). Facilitating patient understanding in the treatment of growth delay. *Clinical Pediatrics, 22*(10), 685–690.

Gross, L.H. (1975). Short, dark, and almost handsome. *Ms, 3,* 75–78.

Gunderson, E.K. (1965). Body size, self evaluation, and military effectiveness. *Journal of Personality and Social Psychology, 2,* 902–906.

Gunderson, E., and Johnson, L.C. (1965). Past experience, self evaluation, and present adjustment. *Journal of Social Psychology, 66,* 241–289.

Hammer, C.H. (1958). A validation study of the Activity Vector Analysis. Unpublished doctoral dissertation, Purdue University.

Hanley, C. (1951). Physique and reputation of junior high school boys. *Child Development, 22,* 247–260.

Harigopal, K. (1979). Self-Ideal Disparity (SID) and adjustment and personality profiles of the high and low SID students. *Journal of Indian Psychology, 2*(1), 45–62.

Harlow, R. (1951). Masculine inadequacy and compensatory development of physique. *Journal of Personality, 19,* 312–333.

Hartl, E.M., Monnelly, E.P., and Elderkin, R.D. (1982). *Physique and delinquent behavior.* New York: Academic Press.

Hartnett, J.J., Bailey, K.G., and Hartley, C.S. (1974). Body height, position, and sex as determinants of personal space. *Journal of Psychology, 87,* 129–136.

Hasler, K.R. and Clarke, W.V. (1968). Reexamination of test-retest reliability of AVA placement analysis scores. *Psychological Reports, 23,* 1035–1038.

Heise, D. (1965). Semantic differential profiles for 1,000 most frequent words. *Psychological Monographs, 601.*

Heise, D. (1969). Some methodological issues in semantic differential research. *Psychological Bulletin, 72,* 406–432.

Hetherington, E.M. and Parke, R.D. (1986). *Child psychology: A contemporary viewpoint* (3d ed.). New York: McGraw-Hill.

Hinckley, E.D. and Rethlingshafer, D. (1951). Value judgements of heights of men by college students. *Journal of Psychology, 31,* 257–262.

Hogan, J. and Quigley, A.M. (1986). Physical standards for employment and the courts. *American Psychologist, 41,* 1193–1217.

Hood, R.B. (1963). A study of the relationships between physique and personality variables measured by the MMPI. *Journal of Personality, 31,* 97–107.

Jenkins, J., Russell, W., and Suci, G. (1958). An atlas of semantic profiles for 360 words. *American Journal of Psychology, 71,* 688–699.

Johnson, L.C. (1956). Body cathexis as a factor in somatic complaints. *Journal of Consulting Psychology, 20,* 145–149.

Jones, M.C. (1957). The later careers of boys who were early- or late-maturers. *Child Development, 28,* 113–128.

Jones, M.C. and Bayley, N. (1950). Physical maturing among boys as related to behavior. *Journal of Educational Psychology, 41,* 129–148.

Jourard, S.M. and Remy, R.M. (1955). Perceived parental attitudes, the self, and body. *Journal of Consulting Psychology, 19,* 364–366.

Jourard, S.M. and Remy, R.M. (1957). Individual variance scores: An index of the degree of differentiation of the self and the body image. *Journal of Clinical Psychology, 13,* 62–66.

Jourard, S.M. and Secord, P.F. (1954). Body size and body cathexis. *Journal of Consulting Psychology, 18,* 184.

Jourard, S.M. and Secord, P.F. (1955). Body cathexis and the ideal female figure. *Journal of Abnormal and Social Psychology, 50,* 243–246.

Kagan, J. and Moss, H.A. (1962). *Birth to maturity.* New York: Wiley.

Kaplan, A.G. and Sedney, M.A. (1980). *Psychology and sex roles.* Boston: Little, Brown and Company.

Katchadourian, H. (1977). *The biology of adolescence.* San Francisco: W.H. Freeman.

Kerlinger, F. (1973). *Foundations of behavioral research* (2d edition). New York: Holt, Rinehart and Winston, Inc.

Keyes, R. (1980). *The height of your life.* New York: Warner Books. GT495·K49

Korda, M. (1975). *Power: How to get it, how to use it.* New York: Random House.

Kretschmer, E. (1936). *Physique and character.* London: Kegan Paul, Trench, Truber, and Co.

Kurtz, D. (1969). *Wall Street Journal, 191,* November 25, p. 1.

La Barre, W. (1954). *The human animal.* Chicago: University of Chicago Press.

Langlois, J.H. and Stephan, C. (1977). The effects of physical attractiveness and ethnicity on children's behavioral attributions and peer preferences. *Child Development, 48,* 1694–1698.

Lerner, R.M. (1969). Some female stereotypes of male body build-behavioral relations. *Perceptual and Motor Skills, 28,* 363–366.

Lerner, R.M., Karagenick, S.A., and Stuart, J.L. (1973). Relations among physical attractiveness, body attitudes and self concepts in male and female college students. *Journal of Psychology, 85,* 119–129.

Lerner, R.M. and Korn, S.J. (1972). The development of body build stereotypes in males. *Child Development, 43,* 908–920.

Lerner, R.M. et al. (1980). Self-concept, self-esteem, and body attitudes among Japanese male and female adolescents. *Child Development, 51*(3), 847–855.

Lowrey, G.H. (1978). *Growth and development of children* (7th ed.). Chicago: Year Book Medical Publishers.

McCandless, B.F. (1960). Rate of development, body builds, and personality. *Psychiatric Research Reports, 13,* 42–57.

Magnussen, M.G. (1958). Body size and body cathexis replicated. *Psychology Newsletter (NYU), 10,* 33–34.

Manual for the Activity Vector Analysis (1973). Providence, RI: Walter V. Clarke Associates, Inc.

Martel, L.F. (1985). Short stature in Caucasian males: Personality correlates and social attribution. Ph.D. dissertation, University of Rhode Island.

Martel, L.F. and Biller, H.B. (1986). In-depth interviews concerning the development of short men. Unpublished study, University of Rhode Island.

Martel, L.F. and Biller, H.B. (1987). Women's perceptions of men as a function of their heights. Unpublished study, University of Rhode Island.

Maslow, A.H. (1952). *Manual for the Security-Insecurity Inventory.* Palo Alto, CA: Consulting Psychologist's Press.

Meredith, H.V. (1978). Research between 1960 and 1970 on the standing height of young children in different parts of the world. In H.W. Reese & L.P. Lipsitt (eds.), *Advances in child development and behavior* Vol. 12. New York: Academic Press.

Merenda, P.F. (1964). Mr. K. and the ideal self. *Perceptual and Motor Skills, 18,* 191–194.

Merenda, P.F. (1968). Cross-cultural perceptions of the ideal self-concept. *International Review of Applied Psychology, 18,* 129–134.

Merenda, P.F. and Clarke, W.V. (1959a). Test-retest reliability of the Activity Vector Analysis. *Psychological Reports, 5,* 27–30.

Merenda, P.F. and Clarke, W.V. (1959b). Factor analysis of a measure of social self. *Psychological Reports, 5,* 597–605.

Merenda, P.F. and Clarke, W.V. (1963). Forced choice vs. free response in personality assessment. *Psychological Reports, 12,* 159–169.

Merenda, P.F. and Clarke, W.V. (1967). Cross-cultural perceptions of the ideal self-concept. *International Review of Applied Psychology, 18*(2), 130–134.

Merenda, P.F., Clarke, W.V., Musiker, H.R., and Kessler, S. (1961). AVA and KPDS as construct validity coordinates. *Journal of Psychological Studies, 12,* 35–42.

Merenda, P.F. and Mohan, J. (1966). Perception of Nehru and the ideal self in Indian culture. *Perceptual and Motor Skills, 22,* 865–866.

Merenda, P.F. and Shapurian, R. (1974). English students' perceptions of health and the ideal self. *Perceptual and Motor Skills, 38,* 1207–1210.

Meyer-Bahlburg, H.F.L. (1985). Psychosocial management of short stature. In D. Shaffer, A.A. Ehrhardt, and L.L. Greenhill (eds.), *The clinical guide to child psychiatry.* New York: Macmillan-Free Press, 110–135.

Meyerson, L. (1963). Somatopsychology of physical disability. In W. Cruikshank (ed.), *Psychology and exceptional children.* Englewood Cliffs, NJ: Prentice-Hall.

Mitchum, R. (1983). Interview in *Esquire Magazine,* February, 99, 52.

Money, J. (1977). The syndrome of house dwarfism: Behavioral data and case report. *American Journal of Diseases in Children, 131,* 508–513.

Moore, D. (1983). Interview in *Time Magazine, 122,* February 21, 70.

Mosel, J.N. (1954). Response reliability and the Activity Vector Analysis. *Journal of Applied Psychology, 38,* 157–158.

Moser, C.A. (1961). *Survey of methods in social investigation.* London: Heinemann.

Mudd, R. (1984). *ABC Evening News,* May 24.

Murphy, G. (1947). *Personality: A biosocial approach to origins and structure.* New York: Harper and Row.

Musiker, H.R. (1958). *AVA and Guilford-Zimmerman.* Providence, RI: Walter V. Clarke Associates, Inc.

Mussen, P.H. (1962). Long term consequents of masculinity of interests in adolescence. *Journal of Consulting Psychology, 26,* 435–440.

Mussen, P.H. and Jones, M.C. (1957). Self-conceptions, motivations, and interpersonal attitudes of late and early maturing boys. *Child Development, 28,* 243–256.

Mussen, P.H. and Jones, M.C. (1958). The behavior inferred motivations of late and early maturing boys. *Child Development, 29,* 61–67.

Naisbett, J. (1984). Interview in *Time Magazine, 125,* July 23, 104.

Nash, J. (1978). *Developmental psychology: A psychobiological approach* (2d ed.), Englewood Cliffs, NJ: Prentice-Hall.

Newsweek (1986). Everybody has scars! *108,* October 13, p. 10.

Nie, N.H. et al. (1975). *Statistical package for the social sciences.* New York: McGraw-Hill.

Novick, M.R. and Lewis, C. (1967). Coefficient alpha and the reliability of composite measurements. *Psychometrica, 32,* 1–15.

Osgood, C.E., Suci, G.J., and Tannenbaum, P.H. (1957). *The measurement of meaning.* Urbana: The University of Illinois Press.

Parten, M. (1966). *Surveys, polls, and samples: Practical procedures.* New York: Cooper Square.

Pearson, K. and Lee, A. (1903). On the laws of inheritance in man: Inheritance of physical characteristics. *Biometrica, 2,* 357–359.

Portnoy, S. (1972). Height as a personality variable in a confrontation situation. Unpublished doctoral dissertation, Temple University.

Prieto, A. and Robbins, M. (1975). Perceptions of height and self esteem. *Perceptual and Motor Skills, 40,* 395–398.

Reich, W. (1945). *Character analysis.* New York: Orgone Institute Press.

Richardson, S.A., Goodman, V., Hastorf, A.H., and Dornbusch, S.A. (1961). Cultural information in reaction to physical disabilities. *American Sociological Review, 26,* 241–247.

Roche, G. (1978). Interview in *American Way 13*, January, 1978, p. 49.

Rosen, G.M. and Ross, A.O. (1968). Relationship of body image to self concept. *Journal of Consulting and Clinical Psychology, 32*, 100.

Rotnam, D.L. (1984). Size vs. age: Ambiguities in parenting short statured children. Paper presented at the Serono Symposium on Psychosocial Aspects of Growth Delay, Arlington, Virginia, October.

Rotnam, D., Cohen, D., Hintz, R., and Genel, M. (1979). When treatment fails: Psychological sequelae of relative "treatment failure" with human growth hormone replacement. *Journal of the American Academy of Child Psychiatry, 19*(3), 505–520.

Rotnam, D., Genel, M., Hintz, R., and Cohen, D. (1977). Personality development in short statured children with growth hormone deficiency. *Journal of the American Academy of Child Psychiatry, 16*(3), 412–426.

Sargent, A.G. (1977). *Beyond sex roles*. St. Paul, MN: West Publishing Co.

Schilder, P. (1935). *The image and appearance of the human body*. London: Kegan Paul.

Schilder, P. (1951). *Brain and personality*. New York: International University Press.

Secord, P.F. (1953). Objectification of word-association procedures by the use of itomonyms: A measure of body cathexis. *Journal of Personality, 21*, 479–495.

Secord, P.F. and Jourard, S.M. (1953). The appraisal of body cathexis: Body cathexis and the self. *Journal of Consulting Psychology, 17*, 343–347.

Seward, G.H. (1946). *Sex and the social order*. New York: McGraw-Hill.

Sheldon, W.H. (1940). *The varieties of human physique: An introduction to constitutional psychology*. New York: Harper and Row.

Sheldon, W.H. (1954). *Atlas of men: A guide for somatotyping the adult male at all ages*. New York: Harper and Row.

Siegel, O. (1982). Personality development in adolescence. In B.B. Wolman (ed.), *Handbook of developmental psychology*. Englewood Cliffs, NJ: Prentice-Hall, 537–548.

Simon, P.V. (1984). Interview in *Playboy, 31*, February, 172.

Singer, J.K. (1976). *Androgeny: Toward a new theory of sexuality*. Garden City, NY: Anchor Press.

Snider, A.J. (1972). Tall and short of success. *Science Digest, 36*, 48–49.

Snider, J.G. and Osgood, C.E., eds. (1969). *Semantic differential technique: A sourcebook*. Chicago: Aldine Press.

Sperling, A.A. (1975). Leisure activity preference of adolescents as related to body image. Ph.D. dissertation, Columbia University.

Spuhler, J.N. (1968). Associative mating with respect to physical characteristics. *Eugenics Quarterly, 15*, 128–140.

SPSSX User's Guide (1983). New York: McGraw-Hill.

Stabler, B., Whitt, J.K., Moreault, D.M., D'ercole, A.J., and Underwood, L.E. (1980). Social judgements of children of short stature. *Psychological Reports, 46*, 743–746.

Staffieri, J.R. (1967). A study of social stereotypes of body image in children. *Journal of Personality and Social Psychology, 7*, 101–104.

Statistical Abstract of the United States (103rd ed.) (1982). Washington, D.C.: United States Department of Commerce.

Steinhausen, H.C. and Stahnke, N. (1976). Psycho-endocrinological studies in dwarfed children and adolescents. *Archives of Diseases of Childhood, 51*, 778–783.

Styzynski, L.E., and Langlois, J.H. (1977). The effects of familiarity on behavioral stereotypes associated with physical attractiveness in young children. *Child Development, 48*, 1137–1141.

Sullivan, H.S. (1974). *Conceptions of modern psychiatry.* Washington, DC: William Alanson White Psychiatric Foundation.

Tabachnick, B.G. and Fidell, L.S. (1983). *Using multivariate statistics.* New York: Harper and Row, Publishers.

Tanner, J.M. (1970). Physical growth. In P.H. Mussen (ed.), *Manual of child psychology,* (3d edition), 77–156.

Tanner, J.M. (1978). *Foetus into man.* Cambridge, MA: Harvard University Press.

Thorndike, E.L. (1920). A constant error in psychological ratings. *Journal of Applied Psychology, 4,* 25.

Tucker, L.A. (1981). Internal structure factor satisfaction and reliability of the body cathexis scale. *Perceptual and Motor Skills, 53*(3), 891–896.

US News and World Report (March 28, 1977). Short people—Are they being discriminated against? *82,* 63–73.

USA Today (July 5, 1984). *3,* 4D.

Walker, R.N. (1962). Body-build and behavior in young children: I. Body-build and nursery school teachers' ratings. *Monograph of the Society for Research in Child Development, 27,* No. 3. (Serial No. 84).

Walker, R.N. (1963). Body-build and behavior in young children: II. Body-build and parents' ratings. *Child Development, 34,* 1–23.

Wallace, R.P. (1941). Apparent personality traits from photographs varied in bodily proportions. *Psychological Bulletin, 38,* 744.

Washburn, W.E. (1962). The effects of physique and intrafamily tension on self-concept in adolescent males. *Journal of Consulting Psychology, 26,* 460–466.

Weatherly, D. (1964). Self perceived rate of physical maturation and personality in late adolescence. *Child Development, 35,* 1197–1210.

Weinberg, M.S. (1968). The problems of midgets and dwarfs and organizational remedies: A study of the Little People of America. *Journal of Health and Social Behavior, 9*(1), 65–71.

Weinberg, J.R. (1960). A further investigation of body cathexis and the self. *Journal of Consulting Psychology, 24,* 277.

Whisler, L. (1957). A study of the descriptive validity of the Activity Vector Analysis. *Journal of Psychology, 43,* 205–223.

Wilson, P.R. (1968). Perceptual distortion of height as a function of ascribed academic status. *Journal of Social Psychology, 74,* 97–102.

Winer, B.J. (1971). *Statistical principles in experimental design* (2d edition). New York: McGraw-Hill Book Co.

Wishon, P.M., Bower, R., and Eller, B. (1983). Childhood Obesity: Prevention and treatment. *Young Children, 39,* 21–28.

Wylie, R.C. (1961). *The self concept: A critical survey of pertinent research literature.* Lincoln: University of Nebraska Press.

Wylie, R.C. (1974). *The self concept,* (rev. ed.). Lincoln: University of Nebraska Press.

Yates, J. and Taylor, J. (1978). Stereotypes for somatotypes: Shared beliefs about Sheldon's physiques. *Psychological Reports, 43*(3), 777–778.

Ziller, R.C. (1973). *The social self.* New York: Pergamon Press.

Ziller, R.C. et al. (1969). Self-esteem: A self-social construct. *Journal of Consulting and Clinical Psychology, 33,* 84–95.

Zion, L. (1965). Body concept as it relates to self concept. *Research Quarterly, 36,* 490–495.

Author Index

Subject Index

Activity factor, 65–67, 76, 95
Activity Vector Analysis, 43, 44–46, 68–72, 80, 81
Adding inches to reported heights, 53
Adolescence, 8, 20, 23–25, 92–93; leisure activities, 14; self-concept and body image, 16–17, 40, 87
Adolescent Growth Study (Berkeley), 24
Aggressiveness, 13, 21, 69, 82, 101
Anger, handling, 14, 88, 91, 92
Anxiety and body image, 16
Assertiveness, 11, 13, 71
Assurance, need for, 70, 71
Athletics and size, 8, 20, 54, 80, 87, 98
Average height, conception of, 62

Basic self, 69–70, 71, 80
Benefits of short stature, 99–100
Body armor, 12
Body cathexis, 5–7; and self-concept, 16–17, 38, 67; see also Body Cathexis Scale
Body Cathexis Scale, 6–7, 43, 44, 56–57, 81, 82
Body image, 41; and parents, 98–99; and self-concept, 15–17, 56–58, 79–81; social comparison, 29
Body satisfaction, 6–8, 79–81
Body types, 2–4; see also Ectomorph; Endomorph; Mesomorph

Children: maturation level, 19–23, teasing of, 6, 19–20
Clinical assessment, 99
Clowning or mascot-adaptational response, 14, 88; and children, 19–20
Compensatory mechanisms, 12–15, 83, 85
Control, locus of, 11

Dating, 26–27, 40; and self-concept, 54, 55, 56, 82
Defensive style, 8, 12–15, 24–35, 39–40
De Gaulle, Charles, 38

Dependence, 70, 71, 80; and maturation timing, 21
Depression, 11, 16
Dominance, 34–35, 82
Draw-A-Person test, 14
Dwarfs, 1, 91

Early maturation, 20–23, 92
Eating disorders, 5
Ectomorphs, 31; and intellectuality, 15; and schizophrenia, 2
Edward Personal Preference Schedule, 22
Emotionality, 11, 69
Endocrine system, 1–2, 99–100
Endomorphs, 2, 31
Ethnic groups, 92
Evaluation factor, 48, 64–65, 67, 75, 95
Eye contact, 34

Family support system, 18, 21, 93–95; see also Parents
Father, absent, 21
Fears, irrational, 13
Fels Research Institute Longitudinal Study, 13
Females, 79–80, 101; and body cathexis, 5, 8; ideal body type, 33; maturation, 22; and men's height, view of, 72–76, 82; and stereotypes of male body, 33
Femininity and body type, 5
Friendship choices, 27, 40

Gaze behavior, 34
Genetic factor, 1–2, 100
Goodness, 64–65
Guidance, need for, 70, 71
Guilford-Zimmerman Scale, 45

Halo effect, 36, 37
Handbook of Developmental Psychology (Siegel), 24
Heterosexual relationship, 8, 25–27, 37, 82, 96; and adolescence, 87; see also Dating; Mating choice
Hiring discrimination, 38

About the Authors

Leslie Martel is currently the consulting psychologist for the in-patient chronic pain management program and the out-patient traumatic brain injury program at Gaylord Hospital in Wallingford, Connecticut. He is also the consulting psychologist for the Gaylord Yale-New Haven Hospital Rehabilitation Center in New Haven, Connecticut, and a consultant to the Connecticut Bureau of Disability Determination in Hartford. In addition, he maintains a private practice in Wallingford and New Haven.

Dr. Martel received his B.S. in psychology with honors and high distinction in 1975 from the University of Michigan in Ann Arbor. He received his Ph.D. in 1985 from the University of Rhode Island. He completed his predoctoral internship in clinical-community psychology in 1981–82 at Yale Medical School, and he spent his postdoctoral years as a clinical psychologist at the Community Health Care Plan, a staff-based health maintenance organization in New Haven and Wallingford.

Henry Biller is professor of psychology at the University of Rhode Island, where he has taught since 1970. He has previously been a faculty member at the University of Massachusetts and at George Peabody College, Vanderbilt University. He has been affiliated with a variety of human service settings for children and families, including Emma Pendleton Bradley Hospital (1970–1980), where he was involved in the training of clinical psychology interns. He is currently a consultant for the group home programs at the John E. Fogarty Center in North Providence, Rhode Island. He received his B.A. in 1962 from Brown University and his Ph.D. in 1967 from Duke University. He is a fellow of the American Psychological Association and is listed in *Who's Who in America*.

Dr. Biller is consulting editor to *Archives of Sexual Behavior* and *Sex Roles*, and his numerous publications include chapters in *Annual Progress in Child Psychiatry and Child Development* (Brunner/Mazel 1971); *The Nebraska Symposium on Motivation* (University of Nebraska Press 1974); *The International Encyclopedia of Neurology, Psychiatry, Psychoanalysis, and Psychology* (Van Nostrand Reinhold 1977); and *The Handbook of Developmental Psychology* (Prentice-Hall 1982).